Related Books of Interest

A Practical Guide to Trusted Computing

by David Challener, Kent Yoder,
Ryan Catherman, David Safford, and
Leendert Van Doorn
ISBN: 0-13-239842-7

Every year, computer security threats become
more severe. Software alone can no longer
adequately defend against them: what's
needed is secure hardware. The Trusted
Platform Module (TPM) makes that possible by
providing a complete, open industry standard
for implementing trusted computing hardware
subsystems in PCs. Already available from
virtually every leading PC manufacturer, TPM
gives software professionals powerful new
ways to protect their customers. Now, there's a
start-to-finish guide for every software professional and security specialist who wants to
utilize this breakthrough security technology.

Authored by innovators who helped create
TPM and implement its leading-edge
products, this practical book covers all facets
of TPM technology: what it can achieve, how
it works, and how to write applications for it.
The authors offer deep, real-world insights
into both TPM and the Trusted Computing
Group (TCG) Software Stack. Then, to
demonstrate how TPM can solve many of
today's most challenging security problems,
they present four start-to-finish case studies,
each with extensive C-based code examples.

Understanding DB2
Learning Visually with Examples, Second Edition

by Raul F. Chong, Xiaomei Wang,
Michael Dang, and Dwaine R. Snow
ISBN: 0-13-158018-3

IBM® DB2® 9 and DB2 9.5 provide breakthrough capabilities for providing Information
on Demand, implementing Web services and
Service Oriented Architecture, and streamlining
information management. *Understanding
DB2: Learning Visually with Examples,
Second Edition*, is the easiest way to master
the latest versions of DB2 and apply their
full power to your business challenges.

Written by four IBM DB2 experts, this book
introduces key concepts with dozens of
examples drawn from the authors' experience
working with DB2 in enterprise environments.
Thoroughly updated for DB2 9.5, it covers
new innovations ranging from manageability to performance and XML support to API
integration. Each concept is presented with
easy-to-understand screenshots, diagrams,
charts, and tables. This book is for everyone
who works with DB2: database administrators, system administrators, developers, and
consultants. With hundreds of well-designed
review questions and answers, it will also
help professionals prepare for the IBM DB2
Certification Exams 730, 731, or 736.

 Listen to the author's podcast at:
ibmpressbooks.com/podcasts

Related Books of Interest

Implementing ITIL Configuration Management

by Larry Klosterboer
ISBN: 0-13-242593-9

The IT Infrastructure Library® (ITIL®) helps you make better technology choices, manages IT more effectively, and drives greater business value from all your IT investments. The core of ITIL is configuration management: the discipline of identifying, tracking, and controlling your IT environment's diverse components to gain accurate and timely information for better decision-making.

Now, there's a practical, start-to-finish guide to ITIL configuration management for every IT leader, manager, and practitioner. ITIL-certified architect and solutions provider Larry Klosterboer helps you establish a clear roadmap for success, customize standard processes to your unique needs, and avoid the pitfalls that stand in your way. You'll learn how to plan your implementation, deploy tools and processes, administer ongoing configuration management tasks, refine ITIL information, and leverage it for competitive advantage. Throughout, Klosterboer demystifies ITIL's jargon and illuminates each technique with real-world advice and examples.

 Listen to the author's podcast at:
ibmpressbooks.com/podcasts

RFID Sourcebook

by Sandip Lahiri
ISBN: 0-13-185137-3

Approaching crucial decisions about Radio Frequency Identification (RFID) technology? This book will help you make choices that maximize the business value of RFID technology and minimize its risks. IBM's Sandip Lahiri, an experienced RFID solution architect, presents up-to-the-minute insight for evaluating RFID; defining optimal strategies, blueprints, and timetables; and deploying systems that deliver what they promise.

Drawing on his experience, Lahiri offers candid assessments of RFID's potential advantages, its technical capabilities and limitations, and its business process implications. He identifies pitfalls that have tripped up early adopters, and shows how to overcome or work around them. This must-have resource can also act as a reference guide to any nontechnical person who wants to know about the technology.

From building business cases to testing tags, this book shares powerful insights into virtually every issue you're likely to face. Whatever your role in RFID strategy, planning, or execution, have Sandip Lahiri's experience and knowledge on your side: You'll dramatically improve your odds of success.

Related Books of Interest

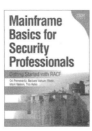

Mainframe Basics for Security Professionals
Getting Started with RACF

by Ori Pomerantz, Barbara Vander Weele,
Mark Nelson, and Tim Hahn
ISBN: 0-13-173856-9

For over 40 years, the IBM mainframe has
been the backbone of the world's largest
enterprises. If you're coming to the IBM System
z® mainframe platform from UNIX®, Linux®,
or Windows®, you need practical guidance
on leveraging its unique security capabilities.
Now, IBM experts have written the first
authoritative book on mainframe security
specifically designed to build on your
experience in other environments.

The authors illuminate the mainframe's
security model and call special attention to
z/OS® security techniques that differ from
UNIX, Linux, and Windows. They thoroughly
introduce IBM's powerful Resource Access
Control Facility (RACF®) security subsystem
and demonstrate how mainframe security
integrates into your enterprise-wide IT security
infrastructure. If you're an experienced system
administrator or security professional, there's
no faster way to extend your expertise into
"big iron" environments.

Lotus Notes Developer's Toolbox
Elliott
ISBN: 0-13-221448-2

IBM Rational Unified Process Reference and Certification Guide
Shuja, Krebs
ISBN: 0-13-156292-4

WebSphere Business Integration Primer
Iyengar, Jessani, Chilanti
ISBN: 0-13-224831-X

Understanding DB2 9 Security
Bond, See, Wong, Chan
ISBN: 0-13-134590-7

Mining the Talk
Spangler, Kreulen
ISBN: 0-13-233953-6

Service-Oriented Architecture (SOA) Compass
Bieberstein, Bose, Fiammante, Jones, Shah
ISBN: 0-13-187002-5

Persistence in the Enterprise
Barcia, Hambrick, Brown, Peterson, Bhogal
ISBN: 0-13-158756-0

Eating the IT Elephant

Eating the IT Elephant

Moving from Greenfield Development to Brownfield

Richard Hopkins
Kevin Jenkins

IBM Press
Pearson plc

Upper Saddle River, NJ • Boston • Indianapolis • San Francisco
New York • Toronto • Montreal • London • Munich • Paris • Madrid
Cape Town • Sydney • Tokyo • Singapore • Mexico City

ibmpressbooks.com

IBM Press Program Managers: Tara Woodman, Ellice Uffer

Cover design: IBM Corporation

Associate Publisher: Greg Wiegand
Marketing Manager: Kourtnaye Sturgeon
Publicist: Heather Fox
Acquisitions Editor: Katherine Bull
Development Editors: Kevin Ferguson, Ginny Bess
Managing Editor: Gina Kanouse
Designer: Alan Clements
Senior Project Editor: Lori Lyons
Copy Editor: Krista Hansing
Indexer: Lisa Stumpf
Compositor: Nonie Ratcliff
Proofreader: Anne Goebel
Manufacturing Buyer: Dan Uhrig

Published by Pearson plc

Publishing as IBM Press

IBM Press offers excellent discounts on this book when ordered in quantity for bulk purchases or special sales, which may include electronic versions and/or custom covers and content particular to your business, training goals, marketing focus, and branding interests. For more information, please contact:

U. S. Corporate and Government Sales
1-800-382-3419
corpsales@pearsontechgroup.com.

For sales outside the U. S., please contact:

International Sales
international@pearsoned.com.

This Book Is Safari Enabled

The Safari, Enabled icon on the cover of your favorite technology book means the book is available through Safari Bookshelf. When you buy this book, you get free access to the online edition for 45 days. Safari Bookshelf is an electronic reference library that lets you easily search thousands of technical books, find code samples, download chapters, and access technical information whenever and wherever you need it.

To gain 45-day Safari Enabled access to this book:

- Go to http://www.awprofessional.com/safarienabled
- Complete the brief registration form
- Enter the coupon code L3LW-38PM-8WA6-9FMJ-ZQUE

If you have difficulty registering on Safari Bookshelf or accessing the online edition, please e-mail customer-service@safaribooksonline.com.

Library of Congress Cataloging-in-Publication Data

Hopkins, Richard.
  Eating the IT elephant : moving from greenfield development to brownfield / Richard Hopkins and Kevin Jenkins.
    p. cm.
  Includes index.
  ISBN 0-13-713012-0 (pbk. : alk. paper) 1. Information technology. 2. Business enterprises—Planning. I. Jenkins, Kevin. II. Title.
  T58.5.H69 2008
  004.068—dc22
                              2008004231

Pearson Education, Inc
Rights and Contracts Department
501 Boylston Street, Suite 900
Boston, MA 02116
Fax (617) 671 3447

ISBN-13: 978-013713012
ISBN-10: 0137130120

Text printed in the United States on recycled paper at R.R. Donnelley in Crawfordsville, Indiana.

First printing May 2008

To Mam, Dad, Lyndsay, and the three best kids in the world: Kirsty, Julia, and Nicholas. They would have preferred a book on real elephants, but at least they approve of the cover.

—R.H.

To Anna, for supporting me through the stressful times of delivering large projects.

—K.J.

Contents

Foreword by Grady Booch xv
Foreword by Chris Winter xvii
Preface xxi
Acknowledgments xvii
About the Authors xxix

Part 1   Introducing Brownfield   1

Chapter 1 ▪ Eating Elephants Is Difficult   3
     Today's Delivery Methods   4
     Why Do Big Projects Fail?   5
     Environmental Complexity   13
     Brownfield Sites Must Be Surveyed   20

Chapter 2 ▪ The Confusion of Tongues   23
     Introducing Brownfield   25
     Key Communication Problems   25
     Overcoming Communication Complexity   34

Chapter 3 ▪ Big-Mouthed Superhero Required   37
     Elephant-Eating Strategies   39
     Consuming the Environment   41

Architecting the Elephant Eater   48
The Elephant Eater in Action   55
The Brownfield Beliefs   60

Chapter 4 ▪ The Trunk Road to the Brain   65
Alternative Wallpapers   66
Invading Hilbert Space   72
Architecture Is the Solution   75
Bridging the Business/IT Gap   79

Chapter 5 ▪ The Mythical Metaman   89
When You Eliminate the Impossible   91
The Long Tail of Business Services   98
Business Attractors for Attractive Businesses   104
The Death of Brownfield   105

Part II   The Elephant Eater   107

Chapter 6 ▪ Abstraction Works Only in a Perfect World   109
Considerations for an Elephant Eater   110
Systems Integration and Engineering Techniques   112
Abstraction Is the Heart of Architecture   118
Do We Need a Grand Unified Tool?   128
The Connoisseur's Guide to Eating Elephants   129

Chapter 7 ▪ Evolution of the Elephant Eater   133
The Sources of Brownfield   134
Isn't This CASE?   138
Isn't This MDA?   139

Chapter 8 ▪ Brownfield Development 143

Agile Waterfalls 144

The Brownfield Development Approach 158

Chapter 9 ▪ Inside the Elephant Eater 165

Looking Inside the Elephant Eater 166

Step 1: Parse View and Identify Patterns 169

Step 2: Merge Views 183

Step 3: Create Transforms 197

Step 4: Generate Artifacts 198

Steps 5.1: Test Artifacts and 5.1a: Identify Generation Faults 199

Step 5.1b: Add and Update Information 199

A Portrait of an Elephant Eater 200

Chapter 10 ▪ Elephant Eater at Work 203

Making the Move to Brownfield 204

Taking the First Step 207

A Better Way to Build Interfaces 207

A Better Way to Build an Enterprise Service Bus 209

The End of Middleware? 211

Evolving a Deployable Enterprise Architecture 212

Index 215

Foreword by Grady Booch

A simple back-of-the-envelope calculation suggests that, worldwide, we produce about 33 billion lines of new or modified code every year. Cumulatively, this means that since the 1940s and '50s (when higher order programming languages began to gain some traction), we've produced somewhere around one trillion source lines of code.

On the one hand, this volume of output suggests that ours is an incredibly vibrant and innovative industry. On the other hand, it's a humbling thought, for through those trillion lines of code, all handcrafted by individual human labor, we've changed the world.

Truth be told, some nontrivial percentage of the 33 billion lines yearly is dead on arrival or so transitory that it's thrown away quickly. Much of that code, however, has a longer half-life, and even some of that code lives after 10, 20, or even 30 or more years. For many developers, the code they write today becomes tomorrow's legacy that their children or their children's children may stare at some day, trying to use it, adapt it, evolve it, asking the question, "What the heck was this developer thinking?"

Greenfield development, quite honestly, is great fun, simply because you get to start with a clean slate and, thus, are not burdened by anything from the past. For the most part, we teach Greenfield development in our schools; furthermore, start-up companies look so much more nimble than their older counterparts because they don't have the millstone of legacy around their necks. Woe be unto the student who enters the real world (it's not like being at the university, unless you move from the college womb to the start-up womb immediately), and woe be unto the start-up company that begins to mature into sustainable development and soon realizes that you can't just start over.

Richard and Kevin introduce us to a reality that's often neglected in our industry: the problem of evolving legacy systems, a domain they call Brownfield development. The typical economically interesting system these days is continuously evolving (you can't shut it off) and ever-growing. The authors identify the root of the problem as that of complexity, and offer an approach that focuses on the fundamentals of abstraction and efficient communication to nibble at this problem of transformation bit by bit. Their model of Views, Inventory, Transforms, and Artifacts offers an approach to reasoning about and executing on the transformation of Brownfield systems. They propose a Brownfield lifecycle involving surveying, engineering, acceptance, and deployment that offers a means of governing this transformation.

As the old saying goes, the way you eat the elephant is one bite at a time. Richard and Kevin bring us to the table with knife and fork and other tools, and show us a way to devour this elephant in the room.

Grady Booch
IBM Fellow
January 2008

Foreword by Chris Winter

I joined the computer industry as a computer programmer, straight from school, in 1969. During a career that has spanned nearly 40 years, I have worked primarily in the area of applications development and systems integration. I wrote my first application in 1969; it was a Computer Aided Design (CAD) graphics application for hardware engineers to design Printed Circuit Boards. This application gave the board designer a tool with the necessary physical rules of the electronic components and how they could be used. In the early 1970s, I developed CAD and other applications to assist building architects in designing large public buildings, such as schools and hospitals. These systems assisted the architects and civil engineers in the design process of the building; by capturing the design, it was possible to produce all the necessary drawings together with the bills of materials for the building.

In the intervening 40 years, I have performed a variety of different roles, including programmer, analyst, designer, architect, project manager, and troubleshooter. The systems I developed were in a broad spectrum of industries, including manufacturing, banking, insurance, retail, utilities, and both local and federal government. Today, I am an IBM Fellow[1] in the IBM Global Business Services division and an active member of the IBM Academy of Technology.[2] My primary responsibility is to technically shape and ensure the technical health of large and complex systems integration and strategic outsourcing programs and bids. I am a Chartered IT Professional (CITP), a Chartered Engineer (CEng), a Fellow of the British Computer Society (FBCS),[3] and a Fellow of the Institution of Engineering and Technology (FIET).[4]

Looking back now on what we tried to achieve with the design and build of electronic circuits and buildings in the early 1970s, I am disappointed and somewhat disillusioned by the IT industry's lack of success in its own adoption of engineering-based methods supported by computer-based tools to architect, design, build, integrate, and test IT systems. In today's world, it would be inconceivable to develop a complex system such as the Airbus 380 without the engineering disciplines and without the engineering tools provided by the IT industry. The IT industry is significantly less mature at adopting engineering techniques to develop its complex systems. It can no longer rely on relatively immature practices often supported by office productivity tools such as word processors, presentation tools, and spreadsheets. The IT industry needs a broader adoption of true engineering-based techniques supported by tools designed for engineers.

It has been my personal experience in recent years that the overall cost and complexity of building bespoke (custom) applications or customizing Commercial Off The Shelf (COTS) packages has increased—as has the risk. On further investigation, it is apparent that it is not the build cost that has increased, but the increase in the size and complexity of the integration of such projects into the systems landscape. From my own recent experience, the ratio of effort of new build to integration is 3:1. For every dollar spent on new functionality, the total cost is four dollars to cutover this function into production. This cost excludes end-user training. In an environment where both size and complexity of the systems landscape are continually increasing, there is a resulting increase in the costs of maintenance. In addition, organizations are burdened with a need to meet increasing levels of legislation and regulation. All of this results in reduced budgets for new development together with decreasing windows of opportunity to deploy new function in the global 24 x 7 service culture. IT innovation is being stifled. The methods and tools that are in use today, albeit limited, are in the main, primarily targeted at Greenfield system's landscapes. The reality is that most organizations in the twenty-first century have an existing, complex systems landscape. When I refer to the systems landscape, I mean both the business and its enabling IT systems. These IT systems, in turn, are comprised of applications and their data deployed on often complex network and computer infrastructure. The documentation of such systems is typically poor and its ongoing maintenance is highly dependent on a small number of knowledgeable "system experts."[5] The IT industry needs a more structured approach to understanding these system landscapes.

This is the reality of the world in which the authors of this book, Richard Hopkins and Kevin Jenkins, and I, architect, design, and implement new systems for our clients in existing complex systems landscapes. It is time that the IT industry face up to the reality of the situation and the need for new development methods and tools that address these issues and take our industry into the twenty-first century.

An important first step in resolving this is to provide a name that describes both the problem and its solution. In the search for a name, the authors have turned to the building industry where new buildings are increasingly being developed on Brownfield[6] sites. This is analogous to the majority of today's new systems that are being developed on Brownfield systems landscapes; it is my experience that more than 90 percent of new development is deployed into a Brownfield environment. The challenges are not restricted to just the transformation of legacy systems, but with the integration into the Brownfield systems landscape itself.

This book describes a new approach to the development of future systems. It is a structured approach that recognizes these challenges, it is based on engineering principles, and it is supported by appropriate tooling. It is specifically designed to solve the challenges of Brownfield development.

Chris Winter
CEng CITP FBCS FIET, IBM Fellow
Member of the IBM Academy of Technology

Foreword Endnotes

[1] "IBM Appoints Six New Fellows Who Explore the Boundaries of Technology." http://www-03.ibm.com/press/us/en/pressrelease/21554. wss, May 2007.

[2] IBM Academy. http://www-03.ibm.com/ibm/academy/index.html.

[3] British Computer Society. http://www.bcs.org/.

[4] The Institution of Engineering and Technology. http://www.theiet.org/.

[5] Lindeque, P. "Why do large IT programmes fail?" http://www.ingenia. org.uk/ingenia/articles.aspx?Index=390, September 2006.

[6] Brownfield is described by the National Association of Realtors® as "The redevelopment of existing urban, suburban, and rural properties already served by infrastructure including 'brownfields' sites, that are or may be contaminated, stimulates growth and improves a community's economic vitality. Development in existing neighborhoods is an approach to growth that can be cost-effective while providing residents with a closer proximity to jobs, public services, and amenities."

Preface

Within every business, there is a desire for rapid change to meet customer demands. Such changes usually involve changing supporting IT systems. When large business changes are required, the accompanying IT changes tend to be significant, too. However, all too often, these big projects hit problems, run over budget, are delayed, or simply get cancelled. Even in 2006, 65% of IT projects failed on one of these counts.[1] Large projects have an even poorer success rate. Such odds are very worrying when the stakes are very high. This book identifies the fundamental issues at the heart of the IT industry's current approaches and provides a new way forward. All people involved in large-scale business and IT change should read this book.

The Day the Elephant Was Born

The IT industry has many key dates, but the introduction in 1964 of IBM's new-generation mainframe, called the System/360, marked the start of a new era. Until that point, buying a new business computer meant rewriting your existing software. The System/360 changed all that with the introduction of a family of compatible computers and associated devices: A program that ran on one would run on any. The industry followed suit with equivalent products, and the nature of IT changed in one fell swoop.

IT investments could now be easily preserved. The programs that ran on the System/360 still run on IBM's mainframe platforms today.

This was an imperceptible change at first, but it was a hugely significant milestone. At this point, IT complexity started accumulating within the enterprise. Systems grew with the business. Thousands of person-years of time, effort, and money flowed into these IT systems. They got complex. They became elephants.

In the meantime, IT fashions came and went. Over the years, the original structured programs have been augmented by object-oriented programming, wrapped by component-based development, and advertised by Service Oriented Architecture (SOA). Each of these movements has had its own strategy for dealing with the complexity, but none ever really took it to heart.

Today's IT systems are so complex that they simply defy everyday comprehension, spilling out of our minds as we try to get our heads around them. Responsibility for maintaining them is split among a variety of skilled groups and myriad products and programs that coexist to support the functions of the enterprise. To deal with this Hydra, we draw high-level architecture diagrams that comfort us by making things look simple. These diagrams are an illusion, a trick, a facade. They are, at best, approximations for easy consumption and high-level communication. At worst, they instill false optimism about our ability to make changes to that complexity.

Such "fluffy cloud" diagrams cannot hide genuine complexity forever. To achieve your business goals and change those systems, you must understand, communicate, and harness the real complexity. No one can understand the whole beast, so vast amounts of well-coordinated teamwork and unambiguous communication are required to complete such tasks. This combination of high levels of complexity and the need for clear communication of that complexity among hundreds of individuals destroys big projects.

Do I Need to Move from Greenfield to Brownfield?

IT systems are generally not implemented on Greenfields any more. The accumulated complexity since 1964 means that the environment for most big IT projects is one of immense challenge, entangled in an almost uncountable number of environmental constraints.

This is the underlying reason for the demise of most large-scale IT projects. Only 30% of large IT projects succeed.

Big projects are usually executed on "contaminated" sites, where you need to be careful of where and how you build; a change in one place can ripple through to other systems in unexpected ways. Such sites are more brown than green, and the IT industry needs to adopt a Brownfield-oriented approach to address them successfully.

This book introduces such a Brownfield approach and explains why current methods are still essentially Greenfield. It is specifically written for people who want to change their business and know that they can do it only by building on what has gone before. If *any* of the following is true, this book is for you:

- You are a CIO, CTO, IT director, project executive, project director, chief architect, or lead analyst who is contemplating a significant change in your IT landscape.
- You cannot afford to replace your whole IT landscape.
- Your systems talk to a fair number of systems outside your direct control.
- You would like to reengineer your existing IT environment so that it will remain flexible for the future.
- You are deeply unhappy with the current failure rates of large IT projects.
- You are contemplating sending a significant part of your IT development and testing work off-shore.

Eating the IT Elephant was written by two full-time Executive IT Architects from IBM who can and have ticked every single one of those boxes on a number of occasions. We have been accountable for the technical direction and day-to-day implementation of some of the largest systems integration and reengineering projects that IBM has undertaken. We believe strongly that existing Greenfield development approaches are an increasingly poor means of addressing today's business problems through IT solutioning. To be blunt, we have a number of years of hard-won experience, and we have grown tired of the recurring problems of IT delivery. In recent years, we have deliberately sought a different approach; the following pages detail the fruits of our labors and that of our colleagues. Heretics we might be, but pragmatists we are also, and, hand on heart, we can say that the insight we share here has significantly accelerated and simplified a number of recent IBM engagements.

We don't think the high failure rate of major IT projects is doing our industry any favors and would like to popularize the approach that has served us well. If we can help mitigate the impact of the unavoidably complex IT environment and knock down some big project communication barriers, we believe that success rate will improve.

A Reader's Digest

This book is not a technical manual nor a cookbook; it does not contain a single line of code, and we have tried to minimize the use of technical diagrams and jargon. This is a book about changing the way we approach large and complex business and IT reengineering projects.

To make the book as accessible to as many people as possible, we have split it into two parts.

Part I is for all readers. Initially, it defines what is wrong with large-scale IT projects and determines the root cause of failure (see Chapters 1, "Eating Elephants Is Difficult," and 2, "The Confusion of Tongues"). The heart of the book (Chapters 3, "Big-Mouthed Superhero Required," and 4, "The Trunk Road to the Brain") concentrate on defining an alternative solution—an Elephant Eater—and the Brownfield approach that goes with it. In Chapter 5, "The Mythical Metaman," we look at the new species of businesses that emerge as a result.

Part II explains the technical and practical aspects of Brownfield for someone who might want to implement such an approach. It starts by analyzing existing Elephant Eating techniques (see Chapter 6, "Abstraction Works Only in a Perfect World") and explains why Brownfield is different (see Chapter 7, "Evolution of the Elephant Eater"). In Chapters 8, "Brownfield Development," and 9, "Inside the Elephant Eater," we look inside the Elephant Eater and at some of the new technologies that have been used to implement it. The book concludes by explaining how the Brownfield approach can be implemented on a project and the benefits it can bring (see Chapter 10, "Elephant Eater at Work").

For those who take the key messages on board, a wealth of technical information has already been published that will enable any organization to adopt the core technologies that we have used (or equivalent ones) to implement Brownfield in their own way (see the "Endnotes" sections of Chapters 8 and 9). We hope that enabling business and IT change via a new project approach, not technology, is at the heart of this book.

Part I: Introducing Brownfield

Chapter 1, "Eating Elephants Is Difficult," introduces the metaphor that performing a large IT project can be compared to eating an elephant. It looks at why big projects fail and provides best practices on how to overcome some of the common reasons for failure.

Chapter 2, "The Confusion of Tongues," explains why this accumulated IT complexity is the root cause of failure, focusing on the human communication problems it creates. It goes on to specifically examine the "great divide" between business and IT that compounds the problem.

Chapter 3, "Big-Mouthed Superhero Required," introduces the core concepts of Brownfield. It looks at how Brownfield can be implemented to create an efficient Elephant Eater.

Chapter 4, "The Trunk Road to the Brain": We despair at IT professionals' inability to communicate as effectively and efficiently as those in other similar professions (such as real architects). Chapter 4 describes how the Brownfield approach combined with the VITA architecture opens up new forms of communication, remote collaboration, and visualization of complex IT problems.

Chapter 5, "The Mythical Metaman": The first part of the book concludes with an examination of the likely impact of Brownfield. It forecasts a new breed of businesses that are infinitely more customer focused and agile than today's and explains how such businesses might come into being.

Part II: The Elephant Eater

Chapter 6, "Abstraction Works Only in a Perfect World": This more technical half of the book opens by defining the characteristics of an Elephant Eater. It considers existing "Elephant Eating" approaches and notes that they tend to compound project difficulties via their extensive use of decomposition and abstraction.

Chapter 7, "Evolution of the Elephant Eater," looks at Brownfield's technical and project roots, and explains its key differences from previous ideas. It ends with some likely scenarios and real-life project examples for which Brownfield has been or could be especially beneficial.

Chapter 8, "Brownfield Development," introduces how the Brownfield development approach can be deployed on a project. It shows how to strike a new balance between Agile- and Waterfall-based development techniques and provides some of the best elements of each. It also describes the core phases of Survey, Engineer, Accept, and Deploy, and states the benefits of the approach.

Chapter 9, "Inside the Elephant Eater": If Chapter 8 described what happens on a Brownfield project, Chapter 9 explains how it happens. This chapter looks inside the workings of an Elephant Eater and explains how it eats the elephant. The chapter also serves as an easy-to-read introduction to the new semantic technologies that underpin Web 2.0 and the semantic web.

Chapter 10, "Elephant Eater at Work": The book concludes with a look at the practical applications of the Elephant Eater and how it can help solve some of today's most difficult IT problems. This chapter includes a summary of the key benefits of the Brownfield approach.

Walking the Brownfields

We hope that you will enjoy reading this book as much as we enjoyed writing it. If you'd like to see more, go to the website www.elephanteaters. org. Additionally, if you would like to see more of the dynamic nature of Brownfield, there are two exhibitions in Second Life. One Second Life site is dedicated to the book [Cypa 30,180,302]. The other Second Life site is dedicated to the use of Brownfield within IBM at [IBM 1 140, 150, 60]. We look forward to meeting you there.

Endnotes

[1] The initial CHAOS report from Standish Group in 1994 reported a 16% success rate for IT projects. This success rate has generally increased over the intervening years. In 2006, Standish Group reported 35% of IT projects being on time and within budget, and meeting user requirements. The only blip in that record appeared in 2004, when failure rates increased. Standish Group explained that in 2004 there were more big projects—they fail more often because they are often forced to abandon iterative development techniques.

In 2007, a rival report to CHAOS by Sauer, Gemino, and Horner Reich looked at 412 projects. It found that more than 65% of IT projects succeeded, but it found no successful projects greater than 200 person-years. This book looks specifically at those large projects.

Hayes, F. *Chaos Is Back.* www.computerworld.com/managementtopics/ management/project/story/0,10801,97283,00.html.

Krigsman, M. *Rearranging the Deck Chairs: IT Project Failures.* http:// blogs.zdnet.com/projectfailures/?p=513.

Rubinstein, D. *Standish Group Report.* www.sdtimes.com/article/ story-20070301-01.html.

Sauer, C., A. Gemino, and B. Horner Reigh. "The Impact and Size and Volatility on IT Project Performance." *Communications of the ACM* 50 no. 11 (November 2007): 79–84.

Acknowledgments

This book would not have been possible without the support and understanding of our families (who don't see us enough at the best of times). In addition, we would like to acknowledge, in alphabetical order, the contribution of the following people or companies:

- **Bob Lojek**—For taking Model Driven Architecture to the next level and for inventing the first plausible attempt at a software Babel Fish.

- **Chris Winter**—A truly inspiring IBM Fellow who believes more in community and the capability of people than anyone else we've met in the industry. Chris was the key driver and technical sponsor behind this work.

- **Christian Hance**—Christian is a project executive in IBM who had enough faith in his architects to enable them to create the first iteration of Brownfield. We are hugely grateful that he also agreed to review this book.

- **Cúram Software**—For introducing us to the practicalities of Model Driven Architecture in the first place.

- **Fred Brooks**—Who calls his seminal work, *The Mythical Man Month,* a bible of software engineering because everyone has heard of it, some have read it, but very few follow it. We hope you do all three and hope this is nearer to a testament than to some apocrypha. We'd like to thank Fred for the quote, "Brownfield is much, much harder than Greenfield, whether software or house remodeling."

- **Ian Hughes**—Probably better known globally as "ePredator potato," Ian introduced us to Second Life and, hopefully, put one more nail into the coffin of PowerPoint-based architectures (see Chapter 4).

- **Ian Scott**—Executive IT architects really shouldn't code, but Ian took the brave step of inheriting the patented approach and code that produced the pictures in Chapter 4. The capabilities of this code are now world-leading, thanks to Ian.

- **IBM**—This book proposes a number of radical ideas; that IBM would endorse the publication of such a book shows Gerstner's Dancing Elephant vision lives on.

- **Mandy Chessell**—For crystallizing the architecture in everyone's heads, patenting it, and unwittingly inventing the acronym VITA. Oh, and the slides—very nice slides.

- **John Tait**—John made us think about the timeline of this book. Why did our gut-feel place the origins of the problem 35 years ago? When we thought about it, we already knew the answer, but we had completely missed the question.

- **Katherine Bull**—We always had enthusiasm, impetus, and drive for the ideas in this book, but Katherine added the same to the publishing process.

- **Kevin Ferguson**—Kevin saved us goodness knows how many days, thanks to his thorough edit and review of our text. No one will suspect we come from Canada.

- **Phil Tetlow**—Phil is the most enthusiastic proponent of all things semantic and inherently complex (including Web Science) and has supported this effort throughout.

- **Our clients**—Last but not least. We can't possibly name you, as the lawyers would undoubtedly get excited, but, without a doubt, the thing that keeps us motivated and innovative is trying to solve the problems of our clients, for their customers. We hope Brownfield will assist in solving some of those intransigent problems you face.

About the Authors

Richard Hopkins and Kevin Jenkins are both executive IT architects in IBM's U.K. services division. They first met in 2002 when Richard hired Kevin to do a few weeks' worth of work performance testing a system for 80,000 concurrent users. The end result of the interview was a spirited argument and solution better than either of them had originally envisaged. They have been collaborating ever since.

They are both members of IBM's U.K. & Ireland Technical Consulting Group, which advises IBM's executives on technical matters. They are also named on the patents that describe IBM's implementation of its Elephant Eater. Brownfield is the result of a number of years of thought and is designed to overcome the deficiencies in the IT industry's way of doing things that the authors have experienced firsthand.

Kevin Jenkins originally found himself in IBM's services division when he returned from a skiing vacation and found that his company had been acquired in his absence. At that time, Kevin was leading the development of major elements of large air traffic control systems for numerous countries.

Since he came into IBM more than 11 years ago, Kevin has moved from air traffic control into other areas. He now leads the successful delivery of systems for governments, financial institutions, and retailers. These solutions include leading the delivery of a major online store system, a pensions portal, and a government customer-management system.

Over that period, Kevin has also performed reviews on a number of projects, and this broad experience of both successes and failures in the industry led him to develop the concepts in this book.

Richard Hopkins is also a long-time member of IBM's services business. In this capacity, he has worked as chief architect for a wide variety of clients around the globe. He has been responsible for delivering systems for governments, banks, insurers, car manufacturers, and software vendors.

During the last 11 years, Richard has successfully led the delivery of a biometric-based national identity card system, a credit card account services system, and a major customer-management system. Tens of thousands of users and millions of customers use his systems every day.

Richard has also been involved in a number of less successful projects. This book draws as heavily on the experience of his failures as it does on his successes.

Outside IBM, Richard chaired the technical definition of the BioAPI standard from 1998 to 2000. BioAPI is the de facto programming standard of the biometrics industry (www.bioapi.org).

He has been resident in Second Life since 2006, where he is known as Turner Boehm. He took the name of Turner because of his love of J. M. W. Turner's oil paintings; to find out why he chose the name Boehm, you will have to read this book!

PART **I**

Introducing Brownfield

Chapter 1 ▪ Eating Elephants Is Difficult

Chapter 2 ▪ The Confusion of Tongues

Chapter 3 ▪ Big-Mouthed Superhero Required

Chapter 4 ▪ The Trunk Road to the Brain

Chapter 5 ▪ The Mythical Metaman

1

Eating Elephants Is Difficult

"Progress is made by lazy men looking for easier ways to do things."

—Robert Heinlein

Chapter Contents

- Today's Delivery Methods   4
- Why Do Big Projects Fail?   5
- Environmental Complexity   13
- Brownfield Sites Must Be Surveyed   20
- Endnotes   21

3

Information technology can now accomplish immensely complex tasks, but despite the IT industry's major strides forward, a disturbing statistic remains: Nearly 70 percent of really big IT projects fail.

This book is all about making these kinds of projects succeed.

In the past 35 years, the computer has changed so much that it is largely unrecognizable and sometimes invisible. I have a small, quiet computer in my living room that can play DVDs, record two digital television channels simultaneously, display my family photos, and play my videos and CDs.

Computers are powerful and everywhere. When I joined IBM, mainstream PCs struggled to stick a few windows on the screen. If you were lucky, your computer talked to a shared file server and provided you with some cute windows that enabled you to look at the green screens where the real work was done. These days, my computer desktop is a panacea of multitasking for documents, virtual worlds, videos, MP3s, e-mail, and instant messaging. I have so many windows doing so many different things that I sometimes think I need another computer to control them all for me.

—R.H.

Today's Delivery Methods

In the past 35 years, the IT industry has changed pretty much everything about how it delivers projects. Rather than starting from scratch with each IT project, huge numbers of standards and techniques are available to draw from. Computer architectures, based on both software and hardware, can be formally recorded in precise and unambiguous ways. Requirements, models, and even logic can be described using standard languages and diagrams. Not much that's written in the multilayered, complex software isn't an object. Supplementing all these IT methods are rigorous and prescriptive approaches for running projects and instilling quality from the start.

However, despite all the advances and standards, the big IT projects don't fail just once in a while: They fail most of the time. Look at the newspapers, or worse still, the trade press: The IT industry has an unenviable reputation for being late, expensive, and inefficient at delivering large projects.

As the Royal Academy of Engineering stated:[1]

> *The overall U.K. spending on IT is projected to be a monumental £22.6 billion (or $45,000,000,000 US dollars). Against this background, it is alarming that significant numbers of complex software and IT projects still fail to deliver key benefits on time and to target cost and specification.*

This report estimates that the success rate of complex projects has reached an unprecedented high of 30 percent from a previously measured low of 15 percent. The industry can hardly be proud of these figures.

Delivering a big IT project is a huge and complex undertaking. It requires sophisticated coordination and strong leadership. The IT industry often measures large projects in terms of the number of person-years expended to complete them. This book is built from the experience gained on a number of projects that took between 300 and 500 person-years, but the information applies to any large IT project. In this book, we compare such projects to eating an elephant: Eating an elephant is difficult, and the dining experience can be disappointing.

Even when the first helping is complete (or the system actually gets delivered), planning some additional courses is normal. Changing, adapting, or augmenting a delivered system is often far more difficult and more costly than expected. This book also considers how to reliably and efficiently achieve such change in a complex environment.

Why Do Big Projects Fail?

In a supposedly mature IT industry, why do big projects often fail, whether through cancellations, missed deadlines, cost overruns, or compromised goals?

Let's assume that the generally well-paid people who execute these IT projects are not stupid. Second, let's assume that they know the proven methods and tools for their job area and are using them properly. This might not be true in all cases, but more experienced staff tends to handle the large and risky projects, so it's not an unreasonable assumption to make.

If people know what they are meant to be doing, perhaps the industry as a whole is immature. Perhaps its best practices are flawed. After all, the IT industry is new compared to older engineering practices, such as building construction.

Still, other modern industries seem to have few of the continuing engineering problems that the IT industry does. Within 35 years of the invention of a new technology, the industries that were spawned are generally working wonders with it. In 1901, the first powered, heavier-than-air airplane took off; by 1936, liquid-fuel rockets and helicopters were being tested and a regular commercial transatlantic airmail service was operating. Thirty-five years is plenty of time to make an entirely new, complex, and very risky technology commercially reliable.

Indeed, taking into account all the improvements that have been made to software engineering over the past 35 years, it is difficult to claim that it is an immature industry. Something other than ineptitude and immaturity is causing the problems.

What can this be? Well, a number of risk areas are known to contribute to project failure, including these:

- Globalization
- Organization and planning
- Project reporting
- Change management
- Induced complexity
- Requirements definition

Demands of Global IT Systems

The world is getting flatter and smaller. IT systems are becoming more global and, thus, must meet new demands. For example, they must cope with vast numbers of users, deal with unpredictable peaks of activity, be available around the clock, and work simultaneously in five languages and a dozen currencies. Meeting these new kinds of demand is challenging, but if these capabilities are identified early enough, they are rarely the core cause of a project's failure.

Organization and Planning

Thanks to politics and commercial constraints, projects are still regularly structured in the wrong way. When this happens, the impact is devastating.

For example, any sizeable project needs a single powerful sponsor or champion who is an interested stakeholder in the success of the delivered project. When multiple people are in charge, the consequences can be disastrous.

On one memorable occasion, a $2,000,000,000 project I worked on was buffeted around by two equally powerful stakeholders from two different organizations for nearly two years. It was a nightmare of conflicting deadlines and requirements. When it came time to make the critical decisions about what the project should do next, the two sponsors could not agree. Finally, the project was given to a single stakeholder from a third organization. This single stakeholder was empowered to make decisions, yet he had an entirely different perspective than the previous two. The result was chaos and lawsuits.

—R.H.

In addition to a single strong sponsor, those who run the project (from commercial, project, and technical perspectives) need to have clear governance arrangements and be empowered to do their jobs. Decision making must be quick and authoritative, but it also must consider all stakeholders who are affected by the decision. Planning must be robust and well engineered, with sensibly sized phases and projects.

Many mistakes can be made in this area. Fortunately, Frederick P. Brooks, Jr. wrote a book about it in 1975 called *The Mythical Man Month*.[2] The authors recommend that everyone leading a big IT project should read it.

Project Reporting

Even if the project is structured correctly, human nature and poor execution can get in the way.

Large organizations are often populated with "bad news diodes"[3] who ensure that senior people hear only what they want to hear. In an electric circuit, a diode allows current to flow in only one direction. In most large organizations and big, expensive projects, human bad news diodes treat news in the same way (see Figure 1.1). Good news flows upward to senior management without resistance, but bad news simply can't get through; it can only sink downward.

Figure 1.1 The bad news diode ensures that bad news sinks without a trace, whereas good news immediately reaches the ears of the highest management.

This is not surprising. Given the size and overheads of big projects, bad news usually means big costs. People often try to cover up and fix any adverse situation until it is too late. No one wants to be associated with thousands of dollars' worth of cost overruns.

Effective managers use project-reporting measures that are difficult to fake, instill a "no blame" culture, and actually walk around project locations talking to all levels of staff, to ensure that all news, good or bad, is flowing around the project.

Change Management

Even if you've managed to get these aspects of your project just right, big projects still have one other inherent problem. Big projects tend to be long.

Given the pace of change in today's businesses, the perfectly formed project is likely to find itself squeezed, distorted, and warped by all kinds of external influences—new business directions, technological updates, or simply newly discovered requirements.

Indeed, as you begin to interfere and interact with the problem you are trying to solve, you will change it. For example, talking to a user about what the system currently does might change that user's perception about what it needs to do. Interacting with the system during testing might overturn those initial perceptions again. Introducing the solution into the environment might cause additional issues.

In IT systems, these unanticipated changes often arise from a lack of understanding that installing a new IT system changes its surroundings. Subsequent changes also might need to be made to existing business procedures and best practices that are not directly part of the solution. This might change people's jobs, their interaction with their customers, or the skills they require.

In the worst case, the business environment into which a system is intended to fit can change during the lifetime of the project or program. The nature of big projects and the time it takes to deliver them could mean that the original problem changes or even disappears if the business changes direction during the solving process. As a result, IT might end up solving last year's business problem, not the current ones.

How project managers analyze the impact of those changes and decide first whether to accept them, and then when and how to absorb them, is a crucial factor of big project success or failure. At the very least, however, the project leaders must be aware of the changes that are happening around them—and, quite often, this is not the case.

Induced Complexity

Advances in technology now mean that the IT technology itself is rarely the cause of a major IT project failure. However, how that technology is put together can sometimes cause problems. Unfortunately, the easy availability of configurable products and off-the-shelf components, combined with the increased tendency to layer software upon more software, can generate unnecessary complexity. This kind of complexity is called *induced complexity*.

Self-discipline within—or a watchful eye over—the technical designers or IT architects is sometimes required, especially in the high-level design stages. At this point, the ease of drawing boxes, clouds, and arrows, and a good dose of brand-new best practices can result in theoretically elegant and flexible architectures that, in reality, can never efficiently be run, operated, or maintained.

We have resurrected several projects that have suffered at the hands of well-meaning but ultimately misguided "fluffy cloud" architects who often have an insatiable desire to apply the latest technologies and ideas. Innovation is good, but it's really not a good idea to innovate everywhere at once.

Instead, IT architects would do well to employ Occam's Razor. Named after the English fourteenth-century logician and Franciscan friar William of Ockham, Occam's Razor holds that the explanation of any problem should make as few assumptions as possible. Assumptions that make no difference to the predictive power of the theory should be shaved off. In other words, the simplest solution that fits the facts is usually the right one.

When applied to IT architecture, this means that any design should be pared to the minimum level of complexity that is required to meet its requirements. Simple is good.

It's always worth asking the following questions of any architecture:

- Am I writing things that I could take from a shelf?
- Do we need that level of abstraction?
- I know product A isn't quite as good as product B at doing that, but because we have to use product A elsewhere anyway, couldn't we use just product A?
- Wouldn't it be simpler if we had only one way of doing that?

On one project, I needed to connect the computer system I was designing to another system in an external organization. The strategic mechanism proposed by the "fluffy cloud" enterprise architects was for the information from our system to be sent in and out of a rabbit warren of connections before the information could be received at its destination. Because of some limitations on the intervening systems, the reliability of the communication could not be guaranteed without a significant amount of extra design and coding. After a minimal amount of investigation, we determined that the two systems that needed to talk were exactly the same type and could be far more securely and efficiently connected directly together.

—R.H.

Requirements Definition

IT projects requirements are often divided into two categories: functional and nonfunctional. Functional requirements describe what the system must do—for example, a user must be able to withdraw money from an account. Functional requirements are often expressed in business process diagrams or use cases, which describe how a user interacts with the system to complete tasks or meet businesses goals.

Unfortunately, nonfunctional requirements are often overlooked. These requirements provide information about the desired characteristics of the system(s) to be built—for example, the system must be available 24 hours a day, 7 days a week. Nonfunctional requirements include response times, performance, availability, manageability, maintainability, and so on. In general, the approach for nonfunctional requirements is less mature and standardized across the IT industry.

The IT industry generally assumes that these two types of requirements encompass all requirements. If they are well documented and managed as described earlier, all is assumed to be well. However, we have observed a third kind of requirement: constraints. Despite being more numerous than the other requirements, constraints are often ignored—until it is too late. We return to constraints in more detail in subsequent chapters.

To illustrate the point, let's eavesdrop on a discussion between a client who is in a hurry and the architect who is designing his dream family home....

LANDOWNER: Thanks for coming over. I'm finding it hard to visualize my new home from those fantastic sketches you sent me, so I thought a site visit would help. The construction firm is lined up to start work next week, so I want to make sure we've got everything right. Otherwise, we won't be able to move in for Christmas.

ARCHITECT: Yes, great idea. I'm glad you liked the drawings. I think the granite facades and the single-story idea will make the most of this view over the valley. A clean and elegant build is just what this site needs. Mind you, looks like quite a steep path to the site. What's the best way down?

LANDOWNER: No, this *is* the site. I said it was on the top of a hill.

ARCHITECT: But we're on a 45-degree slope. You didn't mention the site wasn't flat! I think I'm going to have to make some adjustment to the plans.

The architect speedily makes adjustments to his drawing, dropping his pencil.
Stooping to pick it up, he sees a number of holes leading into the hillside.

ARCHITECT: Hmm, looks like there's some old mine workings, too. Are they safe?

LANDOWNER: Well, they're a couple hundred years old, and they haven't flooded or collapsed yet. They do creak quite a bit, though. I've just discovered a colony of protected lesser-eared cave bats living in one of them, so we're going to have to work around them. To save costs, I think the best thing to do is to move the utility areas of the house down into the unoccupied caverns.

ARCHITECT: Right, okay. I'm going to need a map of the workings to incorporate into the detailed ground plans.

LANDOWNER: No problem. I've got a couple of maps, one from the council's surveyors and the other from the subsidence board.

The landowner hands over some very old-looking maps,
both of which have some tears and holes in them.

ARCHITECT: Er, these maps look completely different. Which one's more accurate?

LANDOWNER: No idea—they kept on digging for another 20 years after those were done.

ARCHITECT: Look, these changes are going to require me to alter the design somewhat. I'll come back next week.

LANDOWNER: Okay, no problem.

One week later.

ARCHITECT: I've worked night and day to put together these plans for the new design. I had to go straight to blueprints, as the building contractors start tomorrow. The house is now on three stories down the hillside, and I've included an underground swimming pool in the largest of the three caverns.

LANDOWNER:	Wow! That sounds great! Never been very good with engineering drawings, though. The roof looks a bit shallow.
ARCHITECT:	That's the side view, and you're looking at it upside down.
LANDOWNER:	Ah, okay. Don't like the look of those windows, either.
ARCHITECT:	That's the stairwell, seen from above.
LANDOWNER:	Right. I think the walls would look better without all those arrows and numbers, too. It's all a little avant garde.
ARCHITECT:	No, those are the dimensions of the building. The walls are still granite.
LANDOWNER:	Well, I'm sure it will look great. Now, you know we're in a hurry, so I guess we'd better start. My mother-in-law is coming down for Halloween, so we might need to make some changes if she doesn't like where you've put the guest room ....

You just know that this build is not going to be a happy experience. The site is a nightmare of subsidence and slopes. The mother-in-law is bound not to like the orientation of her bedroom, and it's pretty clear that the landowner hasn't got the faintest clue what he's been shown. With the construction company arriving next week, you just know that the building is likely to go over budget and probably will not be ready for the Christmas after next.

Environmental Complexity

The architect's initial design had little correlation to the environment in which it was going to sit. Beautiful? Yes. Practical? No. A single-story structure would have been hugely expensive to realize, requiring either major terracing of the hillside or a reengineering of the building by putting it on stilts. Either way, a multistory house built into the hillside was likely a much better solution.

For any complex problem, some degree of analysis and investigation is essential to frame the requirements of the solution and understand its context. In this case, a thorough site survey would have prevented the architect from furiously having to rework his previous plans.

Analysis takes time. Indeed, when building IT systems, analysis typically takes almost as long as building the system. Even then, IT architects seldom do as thorough a job of surveying a site as building architects do. Unfortunately, in IT, relatively little time is spent on the equivalent of a site survey.

This is despite the fact that very few IT projects are delivered on "Greenfield" sites anymore. Most businesses already have a significant and complex IT environment. Some are so complex that they could be considered contaminated or polluted by their complexity. We call such environments *Brownfield* sites.

A site survey enables you to understand this complexity, described in terms of the third kind of requirement we introduced earlier: constraints. These requirements do not specify what the solution must do or how fast it needs to go; they simply define the environment in which it must exist. Constraints massively affect the final solution, but the early requirements phase of any project rarely captures them. This is despite the fact (or perhaps because of the fact) that they far outnumber the number of other requirements put together, as shown in Figure 1.2.

I recently led a project that is fairly typical of the elephantine programs we are discussing. The functional requirements were captured in a 250-page document. The nonfunctional requirements were captured in an 80-page document. The constraints were primarily interface constraints—typically, a 40-page document. Now, that doesn't sound too bad—what were we worried about? Well, the problem was that the documents mentioned were for *each* interface, and there were 250 of them!

—K.J.

All too often, constraints are ignored until the detailed design starts or until the system is being tested for its compatibility with the existing environment. The accumulated effect of these missed requirements is rework, overruns, and, in the worst case—and often in the most complex and expensive situations—project failures.

Boehm's *Software Engineering Economics*[4] provides some startling evidence on how much more it costs to fix such a problem at different stages of the lifecycle. Let's consider, as an example, a complex system-to-system interface that was overlooked as a requirement because no thorough site survey was performed.

Pages

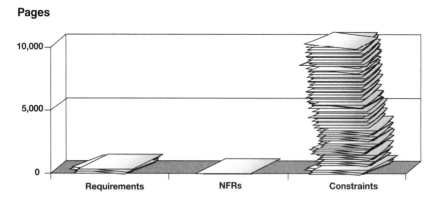

Figure 1.2 The height of the constraints for a big project in terms of paper would be more than 3 feet high. This makes the other requirements look rather inadequate by comparison.

If the omission had been caught at the requirements stage, it might have taken a few days of work and, say, $1,000 to make the update. Now if it isn't caught until the systems are tested together, Boehm's figures suggest that it will cost $50,000 to fix. This is not surprising when you consider the cumulative effects of such a late change. A great deal of documentation would need to be revised at this stage, and a lot of retesting would be required. The project almost certainly would slip.

In the worst of all worlds, the omission might not be noticed until the system went live and things started going awry with customers. At that point, the cost of fixing the requirements defect, Boehm suggests, would be $82,000—and that doesn't include the loss of reputation or consequential damage to the business.

All in all, it's a good idea and good economics to catch defects as early as possible, especially if that defect is a requirement itself. The lack of an IT equivalent of a site survey causes many IT projects to fail.

Unfortunately, no cost-effective, IT industry best practice addresses coping with the existing business and IT environmental complexity that surrounds the solution being delivered. The complexity of the existing IT environment is both unavoidable and very difficult to manage successfully.

Complexity Is Everywhere

Environmental complexity is the almost inevitable end result of many years of IT investment. It is the accumulation of complexity caused by many years of creating, adding, deleting, and updating interconnected and overlapping systems.

This is an almost universal phenomenon, but the IT industry's current best practices, tools, and techniques largely do not recognize it. Almost nothing in the industry toolbox deals with the risks and problems it generates.

This book specifically addresses the problems environmental complexity causes, by introducing a new way of delivering systems specifically designed to deal with both system and environmental complexity.

How Complex Is Complex?

Arguably, environmental complexity started accumulating when the IT industry stopped throwing away everything whenever they bought a new computer. Although the practice sounds bizarre today, before 1964, moving to a new computer required discarding the previous investment in hardware and software, and starting again. The IBM System/360, released in 1964, changed all that by creating a family of computers and attached devices that were compatible with each other.

Over the 40 years or so since the System/360™ and its lookalikes were introduced, most large organizations have invested in and maintained 40 years' worth of information technology complexity. They have accumulated mountains of systems that serve isolated business needs, known as "stove-pipe" systems. After they were installed, they were maintained, extended, used, and abused until their code base became similar to years of solidified lava flow building up on the sides of a volcano. Just as in a real, active volcano, such a system is pretty impossible to shift, no one really likes standing next to one, and only mad people want to poke their heads inside.

The average large business is endowed with a lot of complex computing. The environmental complexity isn't caused by the numbers of computers, the power of those computers, or the size of their data stores—it's caused by the complexity of the code they run, the functional size of the systems.

Function point analysis (now less elegantly known as the IFPUG method[5]), originally proposed in 1979 by Allan Albrecht[6] of IBM, measures how much functionality a system provides to an end user. It also takes into account some of the characteristics (the nonfunctional requirements) of the system. The industry norm for the creation of function points is 10 function points per person-month—that is, a project of 20 people working for a year should result in 2,400 function points.

Surveys of entire organizations can be done to estimate the number of function points present in their system portfolios. How much IT complexity might a bank or government organization have accumulated over the past 40 years? Well, the typical portfolio of applications for a sizeable bank or other large enterprises has been measured at around 500,000 function points. Using the industry norm function point productivity figure[7] means that such a portfolio represents more than 4,000 person-years of effort. It doesn't take much imagination to know that something that has taken this long to build is likely to be exceptionally complex.

Indeed, if you compared the size in person-years of a really large IT project to the size of the business's investment in existing IT complexity, the hugely complex project would be dwarfed, as shown in Figure 1.3.

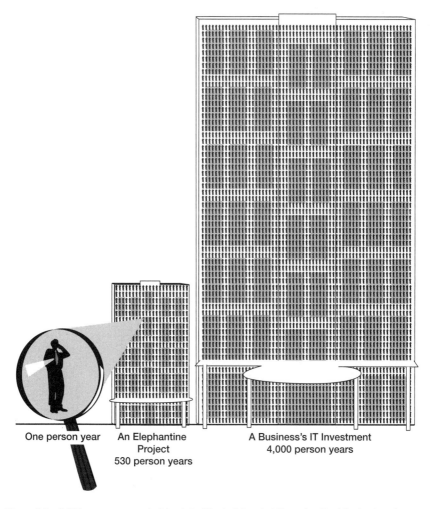

One person year   An Elephantine   A Business's IT Investment
                  Project   4,000 person years
               530 person years

Figure 1.3 A 500 person-year project tends to fill a building, but if we visualized the business's existing IT investment in the same way, it would fill a skyscraper.

A detailed understanding of both is beyond comprehension, but it is precisely this level of understanding that is necessary to ensure that the project will succeed within its environment.

The Effects of Environmental Complexity

The accumulation of complexity in today's IT environments has other impacts besides the failure of large IT projects. The cost of operating and maintaining a high level of IT complexity—in essence, just standing still—becomes more expensive as systems grow larger and older. As a result, only a small part of the spending in an enterprise's IT budget is now devoted to new functionality. In general, IT spending can be split into three main areas:

- **Steady state**—The cost of keeping the existing system going and the maintenance necessary to support the ongoing operations
- **Regulatory compliance**—The changes that are enforced in a business to satisfy new laws and mandatory requirements within an industry
- **Innovation capacity**—The introduction of new capabilities and new technologies into the business

Changes required by legislation are a necessary burden to stay in business. These costs have been rising in recent years partly because of new legislative demands (such as Sarbanes-Oxley compliance), but also because these changes must take place within increasingly complex and difficult-to-maintain systems. Each legislative change makes the IT environment more complex, so future changes and maintenance will cost even more. It is a vicious spiral, as shown in Figure 1.4.

To break this downward spiral and allocate more of the IT budget to new business capabilities, the IT industry must find a better way to maintain and change these large and complex environments.

The Ripple Effect

The most disturbing effect of this environmental complexity is a phenomenon known as the *ripple effect*. This is experienced when a business updates its software or hardware. The business might want a new business function that is offered by the latest software version, or the product the business is using might be going out of support.

Innovation Budget

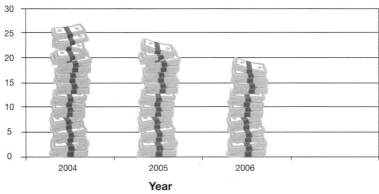

*Proportion of overall IT spend on innovation (%)

Figure 1.4 Gartner's IT Budget Analysis (March 2006) shows a significant yearly decline in the amount of IT budget available for business innovation.[8]

Although the change might seem simple at first, there rarely is such a thing as a nondisruptive change to any nontrivial environment. As the application middleware, database, or operating system version changes, a small but significant ripple is sent out around the environment. Changing one element might require another part of the IT environment to change, to ensure compatibility. Ultimately, these ripples can hit business applications and result in retesting, application changes, or even the need to reintegrate them with their surroundings. Figure 1.5 shows this ripple effect in action.

What started as an apparently small change is suddenly a wide and broad change for many parts of the IT organization. In a typical large enterprise, this could take 6 to 18 months (or more) to complete. In addition, the increasing movement toward globalization and continuous operations limits the time and opportunity to make such changes.

The increasing complexity of existing business, application, and infrastructure environments is thus beginning to slow an organization's capability to change and adapt. All these supposedly independent elements are, in reality, deeply and strongly connected. These ripples are felt hardest when these environmental constraints are poorly defined or captured at the start of the project, with delays and overruns as the results.

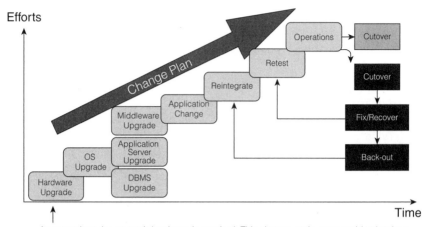

An upgrade to the system's hardware is required. This change, on its own would only take a few hours, but the consequences could be much more significant.

Figure 1.5 A simple change in one area of a complex IT environment can affect other areas, ultimately resulting in a substantial change that requires a business function retest. Such changes can take a long time.

Brownfield Sites Must Be Surveyed

This chapter looked at the frequent causes of failure for large projects. The chances that a big IT project will succeed increase if businesses follow the advice and best practices given in this chapter. However, we have also identified that environmental complexity is the remaining major inhibitor to the success of major IT projects, and this has no obvious answer.

A site survey might enable a business to identify missing or defective requirements early, when they are inexpensive to correct. It could also help a business understand and plan for the ripple effect. Ultimately, a really thorough site survey might help an organization work out how to simplify their IT environment. This could reduce maintenance costs and enable a business to keep up with current legislation more easily. Unfortunately, site surveys almost never happen. This is because using standard IT analysis techniques to perform such a survey across an environment that took nearly 4,000 person-years to build would likely be prohibitively expensive. And as soon as one was conducted, it would be outdated.

The industry needs a new way to conduct major IT projects that takes environmental complexity into account. Such an approach would need to make site surveys cost-effective, practical, and capable of quickly reflecting changes to the environment.

This book is about such an approach. We call it Brownfield to contrast it with the traditional Greenfield development approaches that tend to ignore this complexity. We've borrowed these terms from the construction industry: Brownfield sites are those in which redevelopment or reuse of the site is complicated by existing contaminants. Greenfield sites are clean, previously undeveloped land. Few IT Greenfield sites exist today. Brownfield is not, therefore, a technology or a product, but a new way of executing big IT projects. It is a new way to eat elephants.

In the next chapter, we consider why environmental complexity is such a problem for the IT industry and how we might begin to overcome it.

Endnotes

[1] *The Challenges of Complex IT Projects.* The Royal Academy of Engineering and The British Computer Society. April 2004. Published by The Royal Academy of Engineering London, UK. http://www.bcs.org/server. php?show=conWebDoc.1167

[2] Brooks, Frederick P. *The Mythical Man Month.* Addison-Wesley, 1995.

[3] Birman, Professor Ken. *Integrating the e-Business.* Paper, IFIP/ACM International Conference on Distributed Systems Platforms and Open Distributed Processing, NY/USA, 2000.

[4] Boehm, B.W. *Software Engineering Economics.* Prentice-Hall, Englewood Cliffs, NJ, 1981.

[5] *Function Points Counting Practices Manual—Release 4.1.* International Function Point Users Group (IFPUG), Princeton Junction, NJ, USA, 1999.

[6] Albrecht, Allan J. *Measuring Application Development Productivity.* Proceedings, IBM Applications Development Symposium, CA, USA, 1979.

[7] Jones, Capers. *Applied Software Measurement.* 2nd ed. McGraw-Hill, Inc. New York, NY, USA, 1996.

[8] Gartner Executive Programs (EXP). *Gartner CIO Survey.* Gartner Inc, Stamford, CT/USA, 2006.

2

The Confusion of Tongues

*"The problem with communication ... is the illusion that it
has been accomplished."*
—George Bernard Shaw

Chapter Contents

- Introducing Brownfield   25
- Key Communication Problems   25
- Overcoming Communication Complexity   34
- Endnotes   35

In Chapter 1, "Eating Elephants Is Difficult," we introduced IT environmental complexity as the major roadblock for the successful delivery of big IT projects. Not only are the projects themselves complex, but the environments into which they deliver their new systems are, too.

Why is complexity such an inhibitor for success? It's not the actual complexity that causes the problem—it is understanding and communicating that complexity. Consider the parable of the blind men and the elephant—a story so old, its origin is unclear:

Once upon a time, not so long ago, three blind men were happily sitting together on the park bench that they frequented every day. From that bench, they talked with each other and heard the world go by.

One day, they heard the crunch of huge footprints. Not knowing what approached, they became alarmed.

A passerby saw their alarm and reassured them, "The circus is in town. What you hear are their elephants strolling through the park." None of the men had ever been near an elephant—at the zoo, they were on the other side of a big ditch—so the kind passerby led them to the nearest beast.

One man was led to the side of its head, the next to its side, and the last to its trunk. Each raced his hands over the amazing animal. The men filled their heads with their experience of what an elephant was really like.

After they returned to their bench, they compared notes. "It was beautiful and delicate, just like a huge sail," said the first man, who had held its ear. "No, no!" said the second. "It was more like a huge wall of flesh." "Rubbish!" said the third, who had held the trunk. "An elephant is clearly some kind of snake."

An argument ensued, but each man knew he was right and refused to concede. The bench became a less pleasant place to be.

The parable provides an important lesson in holism and ensuring that you understand the whole problem. In many regards, this parable is at the heart of one of the key messages in this book—but in our problem, there are not three blind men, but more than a hundred people, each with his or her own disconnected view of the elephant and an absolute belief that his or her view of the problem is the right one.

Introducing Brownfield

By definition, any large project is executed by a large number of people with different roles and responsibilities. Each person needs to coordinate his or her activities and outputs with those of the other people working on the project. This occurs through varying degrees of formality, including documents, conversations, plans, notice boards, e-mails, methods, and even instant messages. As the project gets larger and more complex, more people are needed to handle that complexity, and the amount of communication grows.

Fred Brooks identified this problem in 1975 in his seminal work on software engineering, *The Mythical Man Month*. While delivering the hugely complex OS/360 operating system[1] that ran IBM's new generation of mainframes, Brooks noticed that adding more people to a project increased the communication overhead and actually reduced productivity. Adding people to a late software project to speed it up actually makes it later. This observation has become known as Brooks's Law.

Of course, Brooks had it easy. All he had to do was control communication within his own local team. Today's environments are more complex: We rarely have the opportunity to build a complete, self-contained system on a Greenfield site with a local team. Whatever we build must satisfy the new capabilities required and also use the information and facilities that are present in the existing IT environment. For example, for any new system that must communicate with other existing systems, existing users must be able to operate it, and the existing maintenance staff must be able to support it. Each of those areas (business analysts looking at new functions, data modelers and database administrators looking at existing data and other system owners, and so on) requires us to find, talk to, and establish a working relationship with yet another group of people. This is increasingly difficult when groups are located in separate time zones.

Key Communication Problems

With considerable communication difficulties arising between groups within projects, and between projects and their surrounding environments, how can we improve these areas? To solve these kinds of problems, we need to better understand the issues of complex communication. In the next section, we analyze why communication fails and what we can do to improve it.

Introducing Views

Elephantine projects, by definition, involve a lot of people. Clearly, not everyone on the project can understand everything that is going on. Each person tends to concentrate on a particular view of the project.

For example, a project director who is responsible for the entire project's success might have a very broad and shallow view, focused on the major commercial aspects and major deadlines of the project. A programmer who is responsible for writing a component of the overall solution might have a small and contained view, but this person would understand this area better than anyone else on the project. The chief architect might need to understand a little bit of the commercial and resourcing view, but would also need to know how that programmer's component fits into the whole solution; this person's view would be exceptionally broad but necessarily superficial.

These perspectives are central to the Brownfield approach that we outline in this book. Throughout the book, we call them *Views*. Views are formal, bounded perspectives of an overall project or problem. Views are typically maintained by a single person or a like-minded, similarly skilled team. They can range from plans, estimates, or designs, to code or definitions of business processes. Views are the components from which projects are built.

Views can vary drastically in breadth and depth, but they typically contain a similar amount of information. We believe that Views generally become widely adopted and successful if they limit their scope to the amount of information that the average human brain can realistically and reliably store and process.

Looking across multiple projects, heuristic rules suggest that we can express the size of a View more precisely in terms of the function points introduced in Chapter 1. We believe that a successful View typically contains no more than 2,000 function points.[2] To determine this, we have used a number of estimating techniques, including these:

- Dividing the number of function points in a variety of large projects by the number of people who, as a group, are meant to understand all of it

- Asking individuals to remember the largest project in which they knew all the relevant details

When a large project might deliver tens of thousands of function points in an environment that contains 500,000 function points, the implications of this limitation should be obvious.

Using this rationale, it should also be clear that the size of the project and the output environment can create communication problems. To understand the real environment (or Brownfield site) that you are delivering into at the level of detail that will allow your integration to work, you need access to many Views. Few, if any, of the people on your project will maintain or understand those environmental Views.

Unfortunately, as the responsibilities on the project are divided among people, the "2,000 function point" Views they choose to do their jobs can never be entirely independent. The definition of the hardware that runs the project is inextricably linked to the design of the business application and the supporting software that has been chosen. Each of the Views partially overlaps the others. These three overlapping Views of hardware, application design, and supporting software are all linked by a performance model View that describes how the system will behave when users execute their business tasks on the system. These business tasks are described in a business process model View, which, in turn, is linked... and so on.

This tendency to segment the whole into a complex network of intersecting and overlapping Views causes three types of communication difficulties:

- Inconsistency
- Ambiguity
- Parochialism

Inconsistency

Inconsistency arises because the Views overlap. A well-engineered project aims to remove duplicate information across Views, but some duplication is inevitable. For example, duplication is required so that we can trace information from one document to another. (Some common information must exist to make the link.) In other cases, we can summarize or decompose information between documents.

Documenting the requirements and solution of a big project can produce large amounts of information. As you saw in Chapter 1, the requirements themselves (including functional, nonfunctional, and constraints) can easily be more than 10,000 pages. Most projects involve writing requirements documents first, followed by architecture and design documents; then the solution is coded and tested. A network of ancillary documents supports each of these documents—plans, estimating models, and status reports that support the overall management of the project. Clearly, if the requirements change significantly when the coding is being performed, it produces a cumulative effect on all the intervening and ancillary documentation.

For example, if a programmer notices during the project's coding stage that the system under construction needs to talk to another system, many previously written documents will need to be updated, including plans, architectures, designs, and estimation models. In addition, many people will need to know about those changes so that they can act on them. Whenever the shared information is updated in one place, it must be updated in all the other places it is found. Unfortunately, this requires everyone to know where the information is duplicated and to follow a rigorous process.

As the project and its environment grow more complex, these effects become more pronounced and more difficult to efficiently administer. As complexity grows, the number of Views that are required to encompass the complexity grows. As the number of Views grows, the number of potential connections between them grows. The more connections exist, the greater the burden of keeping everything in step and the reduced likelihood that it actually will happen. This growth in connections is exponential instead of linear in nature because every new View could conceivably be connected to every previous View. In reality, each new View is connected to only a small proportion of the other Views, but even in such a model, the communication overhead grows faster than the size of the project.

Ultimately, either the manual process of maintaining these tens of thousands of pages of paper documents breaks, or the overhead it causes slows the project to a snail's pace. In either case, the ability to manage the project's and the surrounding environment's complexity is lost. The project is undermined by the inability to efficiently manage the complexity and communicate it.

Therefore, despite the dire warning of *The Mythical Man Month,* productivity on such large projects is almost always overestimated. As a result, project managers still tend to throw people at the problem when things go slower than expected, which can result in a downward spiral and project failure. To solve this problem, any Brownfield-oriented approach needs to remove the inconsistency issue between Views.

Ambiguity

The English language is imprecise and conducive to miscommunication. Much English-language humor is based on its capability to be ambiguous. As Groucho Marx famously said, "I shot an elephant in my pajamas. What he was doing in my pajamas, I'll never know."

A quick look in a thesaurus confirms that many individual words are ambiguous. If something is *hard,* does that mean that it is difficult or that it would hurt if you ran into it?

In addition, our sentence structures can be ambiguous. Does *complex project development* mean "the task of development is complex on the project" or "the development of a complex project"?

Projects can have very long chains of communication, and any degree of ambiguity can be amplified as the message flows through the project. In "bad news diode" cultures such as the ones described in Chapter 1, this can be exploited. Indeed, we observed one example in which the message issued to the project was diametrically opposed to the one issued by the project sponsor. Just two layers of management exploited a degree of unintentional ambiguity in the original message.

With its lack of gender and noun/verb agreements, the English language almost encourages miscommunication. Anyone who has ever played the whisper game—in which a message is passed between a group, with each participant repeating the original phrase—knows that, after a few exchanges, the meaning of the phrase can change completely. Such information decay is not the result of participants intentionally exploiting the language's ambiguity or deliberate lack of precision; it is just an everyday fact of communication failure. Probably the most famous example of this comes from English military history in World War I. The original message issued was "Send reinforcements—we're going to advance." After being relayed a number of times, the message received was "Send three and four pence[3]—we're going to a dance." Not surprisingly, the reinforcements did not arrive in time for the push forward.

To ensure that messages are understood, we often need to supplement our words with tone of voice and body language. Good face-to-face communicators also test common understanding during a conversation. Unfortunately, face-to-face communication is not always possible on large projects. On such projects, most conversation is asynchronous, in that information is issued without expecting any immediate acknowledgment. Whether e-mail based or via lengthy documents, the communication is essentially "fire and forget." Yes, you might have an opportunity to review the document, or you might be able to question the e-mail, but these acts are the exception, not the rule. After a document or instruction is issued, it is used and reinterpreted without question.

This removal of real-time, nonverbal feedback often occurs when teams are geographically separated. The loss of body language and signals can cause misunderstandings because words and sentence structures can be ambiguous. Of course, this is becoming an ever-increasing problem on IT projects whose resources are spread across the globe.

Parochialism

Parochialism is a natural outcome of dividing a project into multiple areas of responsibility and asking each part to ensure the success of its own area. As a result, people consider only the elements of the problem or solution that are directly relevant to their View, and they consider themselves to be only a small part of the overall problem.

This kind of behavior is often endemic in large organizations. When Lou Gerstner became chairman of IBM, he was horrified by the parochial management style. He immediately changed the incentive scheme of his senior management team so that managers were rewarded by overall corporation success instead of primarily by the success of their part of the organization.

Parochialism kills projects because the success of only one View means nothing—only the success of the conglomeration of Views can actually deliver success.

Parochialism is not caused only by dividing responsibilities into specific Views. It is even more likely to arise when teams are geographically separated. In *Peopleware*,[4] Tom DeMarco and Timothy Lister list physical separation as a key technique for achieving teamicide—their term for the ability to prevent a successful team from forming.

The separation need not be large. On one project we observed, almost no communication occurred between the application architects and the middleware architects. This lack of coordination led to misunderstandings and overlaps and underlaps of Views, resulting in high levels of inconsistency. Ultimately, the project became a dysfunctional and highly fractious one that failed to deliver. Unbelievably, the teams who never spoke were in the same building, on separate floors. The physical distance between them wasn't more than 12 feet, but it was enough to derail the entire project.

Splitting teams across buildings occurs often these days. Advances in worldwide communication and access to inexpensive but highly skilled labor across multiple continents means projects many times are split across the globe.

If communication between floors is difficult, then communication via long-distance phone calls, between cultures and time zones, is almost certain to cause communication difficulties. Projects are sometimes deliberately geographically split so that they can achieve around-the-clock effort—that is, a team somewhere in the world is always working on the project. These projects experience all kinds of communication issues. For example, it is impossible to schedule a convenient time for a joint teleconference. Such problems lead to intense parochialism, as the bond to the local team becomes far stronger than the bond to the project.

One relatively small project that I recently reviewed had its project manager in New Zealand, its application management in India, and its design team in New York—and it reported to a business based in London. The systems were located in a number of data centers around the globe. Each was maintained by a different company. Not everything ran as smoothly as it could.

At the same customer, I worked with another team that was truly based around the globe. Some people were in Texas, others in the U.K., one or two in Asia, and the leader of the group was in Australia. The team could meet in person only once a year, and it was pretty clear that most of the individuals had a stronger network and team spirit built around their previous local roles than they did with their geographically dispersed team.

—R.H.

Language Speciation

The ultimate form of parochialism is the creation of a private language that only your own area of the project can understand.

Even when people are in the same room, the IT industry is so full of acronyms and specialist terms that people who have slightly different perspectives or backgrounds often can't understand what is being said. This trend toward language divergence is apparent in all aspects of human life.

Another such group of like-minded individuals is stock brokers. When stock brokers talk, they speak a different language than the rest of the world. Most of the words seem familiar, but they are put together in strange ways that are difficult to understand for an outsider. This also occurs with businessmen, IT personnel, and even children. All of these groups use words or terms to mean different things, or they use acronyms as words. This is done to provide clarity and simplify communication within the group, but it creates a barrier to those outside. For example, teenagers' text messaging is an entirely new experience:

> f u tnk dat theres NP n transl8N thN l%k @ yr kids txt msgs. Itz a diFrent wrld n lang.
>
> *Translation:* If you think that there is no problem in translation, then look at your kid's text messages. It is a different world in language.

Looking at the original text message, you might be able to deduce most of the words, but this was a very simple example. It doesn't contain any of the code words that you couldn't really deduce, such as "CD9" for "Code 9," which translates to "Parents Are Around," or "MOS" for "Mom Over Shoulder."

Linguists have a theory known as mosaic language zones[5] that explains this proliferation of languages. The mosaic theory suggests that in conditions of strong competition, languages tend to mutate and speciate. This divergence into many different tongues is thought to be a way to detect outsiders and enforce a sense of security. The language or dialect becomes a badge of group membership. Private languages are endemic in the IT industry, and although they might offer a small advantage in terms of communication efficiency within the same immediate group, they can cause many problems across a large project.

Private languages are a natural outcome of having highly specialized jobs in a highly competitive industry. It is unlikely that we can remove this blocker for better communication—and human nature might make it impossible. If this is the case, the Brownfield approach must embrace the need for private languages without impairing our ability to communicate between groups.

The Business/IT Gap

Perhaps the most disturbing and worrisome manifestation of parochialism is that business and IT do not share the same language. As a result, business and IT frequently misunderstand each other. Project requirements are lost in translation, and the distance between the business and IT often makes it difficult to resolve these misunderstandings. To resolve this, it must be possible to describe both the problem that the project will address and the problem's proposed solution in a way that is meaningful to both the business and IT worlds.

Unfortunately, during the past 20 years, business and IT have moved farther apart. A decision made in the boardroom is conveyed to the IT department as a request to be fulfilled. No real dialogue exists. Confirming the requirements is difficult when virtually no two-way communication occurs.

Compounding this situation is the lack of success in delivering large projects to enable the accelerated business change that is necessary to be competitive. Little common language exists between business and IT, so the two have precious little to talk about other than high-level requirements, deadlines, milestones, and budgets. These terms form a very limited common ground.

Service Oriented Architecture (SOA) is beginning to soften this standoff. SOA breaks down business software into granular, business function-oriented chunks that organizations can flexibly combine to create new business and IT capabilities. When applied correctly, SOA aligns the services that the business wants to provide to its customers with the IT services that underpin them. In addition, the IT services are expressed in business terms instead of in terms of the underlying application or technology. This alignment provides a common, business-focused but precise language for the business and IT worlds to jointly define problems and solutions.

At the same time as SOA was introduced, some of the software-engineering techniques that have evolved over the past 20 years are beginning to be applied to reengineer the business itself. IBM's component business modeling is an excellent example that uses the philosophy of designing large systems to conceptually break the business into small, largely self-contained capabilities. The organization then can determine whether duplication of capability exists within the organization. It is also possible to see which areas are unique and core to business success, and which areas are less critical. Those less critical areas could be sold off or outsourced.

This convergence of business modeling and IT modeling provides an opportunity for the business and IT perspectives to align. This clearly can improve communications and, ultimately, result in a better ability to provide more aligned solutions to business problems.

We summarize this principle in a Brownfield Belief. The Brownfield Beliefs are a set of directives that summarize the difference between traditional Greenfield and Brownfield techniques. The first principle is this:

- Make Business and IT Indivisible

SOA provides a fantastic end goal for this principle, but many businesses struggle with the migration from their existing, highly complex Brownfield environments to the new, rationalized, and business-oriented services environments.

Therefore, our Brownfield approach aims to remove inconsistency and ambiguity from communication and to enable the establishment of a language that spans both business and IT.

Overcoming Communication Complexity

In this chapter, you have seen that inconsistency, ambiguity, and parochialism are unfortunate but natural aspects of how we communicate. In any situation when a complex task has to be divided into a number of different tasks, you are likely to observe such problems, whether you are working in civil engineering or IT engineering. When the project involves the highly abstract concepts of software design (as opposed to bricks and mortar), the problems are exaggerated because the core complexity of the thing you are trying to build is itself expressed in a language (the code that the system runs).

To cope with the accumulated complexity of today's systems and deliver projects reliably and efficiently, we need an approach that absorbs complexity and copes with the inherent communication problems that people face. This cacophony of communication (or lack of communication) is illustrated by the small subset shown in Figure 2.1. To this small subset, we could add many different types of code, models, requirements, process definitions, methods, and tools. Each one has its own largely private language preventing communication and allowing the gaps and inconsistencies between the Views to be poorly understood.

We have concluded that, when faced with a hugely complex environment and a massive program of change, the only way to cope is to build something to handle the complexity for us. We need a machine to eat our elephant. We need an Elephant Eater. In the next chapter, we consider how such a beast might be built.

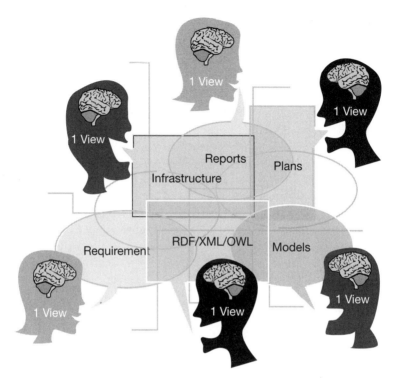

Figure 2.1 Many overlapping Views in multiple languages are needed to deliver a big project. These overlaps permit inconsistency and ambiguity to impede progress. In the worst case, people adopt a parochial perspective—as a result, projects fail.

Endnotes

[1] OS/360 was the operating software for the System/360. OS/360 insulated the business software from needing to understand the details of the System/360 hardware that it ran on. This made it easy to keep the business software unchanged as the hardware changed. Much of the IT environmental complexity we deal with today stems from the success of OS/360 in enabling this.

[2] In reality, the 2,000 function points is a very rough approximation. According to the strict rules that govern function points, a View that consists of hundreds of business rules might contain no function points. Our intent is to try to describe the size of the View so that we can relate

it to project size. In reality, a View could be a logical data model, a number of use cases, or even the formal description of a number of IT components.

3   Three and four pence means 3 shillings and 4 pence. This translates into 19 old pence, which is approximately 8 new pence, or 16 cents.

4   DeMarco, Tom, and Timothy Lister. *Peopleware.* Dorset House Publishing, New York, USA, 1987.

5   In *Before the Dawn: Recovering the Lost History of Our Ancestors* (Penguin Press, New York, 2006), Nicholas Wade suggests that mosaic language zones, such as New Guinea, where 1,200 languages (one-fifth of the world total) exist in an area a quarter of the size of the mainland United States, are the result of fast, socially driven language mutations. We believe that we see the same effect in the highly competitive IT industry.

3

Big-Mouthed Superhero Required

"Out of intense complexities, intense simplicities emerge."
—Winston Churchill

Chapter Contents

- Elephant-Eating Strategies 39
- Consuming the Environment 41
- Architecting the Elephant Eater 48
- The Elephant Eater in Action 55
- The Brownfield Beliefs 60
- Endnotes 64

In the worst situations when communications break down and projects repeatedly fail, IT becomes a blocker, not an enabler, of change. Projects can become too large and complex to succeed, not only because of their internal complexity, but also because of the unavoidable complexity of the surrounding IT and the users' environment. Information about those external environments and expert knowledge about them is often nonexistent or in short supply. In the worst situations, the elephant becomes frozen. As a result, the business becomes frozen, too—it cannot move.

The rest of this book is about thawing and eating those elephants.

This book intends to show that the way we deliver projects—the way we consume elephants—is inherently wrong. Indeed, as we continue the earlier metaphor, illustrated in Figure 3.1, we believe it is especially inadvisable to eat frozen elephants.

Figure 3.1 We were concerned that a knife and fork might not be sufficient for the job.

Elephant-Eating Strategies

An organization can use three possible methods to eat an elephant:

- A single person can eat the elephant (see Figure 3.2). This solves most of the communication problems, but it would take a very long time.

Figure 3.2 Bill's son looks on in adoration as his dad continues his life's work. One day, all this will be his.

- Use a number of stages and a number of people per stage, as shown in Figure 3.3. The IT industry currently uses this solution. The elephant will get eaten a lot faster than with the previous option, although the people will need a lot of management and coordination to direct who should eat which parts and when.

- In desperation, we could look for a superhero (see Figure 3.4) with a very large mouth. This means that, in theory, the elephant could get eaten a lot faster. Unfortunately, most of the superheroes are too busy saving the world to take the time to eat an elephant.

Figure 3.3 Bill's approach was eventually shelved in favor of a more streamlined approach.

Figure 3.4 Coordination between the "chewing" and "swallowing" departments broke down after a few months—we're now in search of a big-mouthed superhero.

Clearly, the first option is not viable. Although an elephant could be eaten that way, a business that waited that long for an IT solution to arrive would go out of business. The second option has all the communication and coordination problems discussed in Chapter 2, "The Confusion of Tongues." Perhaps the third idea, although fanciful, has some merit. Clearly, the possibility of finding an IT superhero who could somehow swallow all that complexity is out of the question—no such individual exists. But perhaps it would be possible to build an elephant-eating machine. Is it possible to build an Elephant Eater that could accomplish the same task?

We faced all the problems we've talked about so far in this book during one particularly large and complex government project. Not only was the environment complex, but the systems that needed to be built were complex, too. Each system had thousands of business rules and tens of thousands of users who used the system every day. In addition, these systems were the very heart of the organization. They talked to virtually every other system across their IT estate (and many beyond). If these systems failed, the government's advisors confidently predicted riots on the streets within a week. If an Elephant Eater was ever needed, it was needed now. So we decided to build one.

—R.H. and K.J.

Consuming the Environment

Any Elephant Eater needs to directly address the problems with the complexity and communication identified in the previous chapter. This involves addressing the reality of ambiguous communication, parochialism, and private languages that prevail in large projects. This also involves addressing the need for communication among multiple distributed teams, both on and off the project, with overlapping responsibilities.

Overcoming Inconsistency and Ambiguity

First, we need to remove inconsistency between Views. To achieve this, the Elephant Eater needs to consume all Views on the project. As new Views are fed into the Elephant Eater, it checks them for any inconsistency with the other Views already entered. If the information inserted is inconsistent or contradicts the information already in the Elephant Eater, this needs to be corrected before the information is fed in.

The key question is, how can this be done? Surely this means that the information being fed in needs to be precise and unambiguous; otherwise, how will the Elephant Eater know whether it is consistent? This is a very fair point. To explain how this is done, we introduce three formal terms that help describe the core elements of communication:

- **Syntax**—The study of the rules or "patterned relations" that govern the way words combine to form phrases and the way phrases combine to form sentences
- **Semantics**—The aspects of meaning that are expressed in a language, code, or other form of representation
- **Context**—Important ancillary information for understanding the meaning being conveyed

To put it simply, we communicate at all levels by using syntax. But to get the full meaning of any communication, it is necessary to understand the semantics of its use and the context in which it is used.

Consider the word "check." A check is an order for a bank to make payment of money from a bank account to some other party. A check could also be the bill in a restaurant. When talking about a process, it could be an inspection or verification step. At a tailor, it could be a pattern on a shirt. In playing chess, it could mean a direct attack on the king...and the list goes on. Of course, these are just its meanings as a noun. Thanks to the unusual flexibility of the English language, the word can also be used as a verb.

How is it possible to ascertain what meaning of the word is being used? Sometimes it's impossible to be certain, but, more often than not, you can determine the meaning (that is, the semantics) by the surrounding context. For the Elephant Eater to be able to clarify all those Views, it needs to have some understanding of syntax, semantics, and context.

The Syntax Wars

Historically, the IT industry has experienced many syntactic difficulties. In the earliest days, different flavors of common computer languages existed. A program that ran in one environment might need to be changed to run in a different one. The syntax or rule structure of implementations using the same computer language might be subtly different. Today the syntax of languages is highly standardized. The programs used to create computer programs (editors) recognize the required syntax and even helpfully fill in the rest of the line or correct your program's syntax.

If you've seen green wavy lines appear under your sentences as you type in Microsoft® Word, you might be familiar with its grammar checker, which has a pretty impressive knowledge of English syntax.

Of course, the IT industry's syntax problems went well beyond computing languages. Reading program code to understand the design of a system is a time-consuming business, so the computer industry uses "models" to record the core features and structure of complex systems. These models are usually recorded as diagrams that normally consist of two-dimensional boxes and lines.

Today's system designs are created and maintained by these models. However, would a diagram that makes sense to you make as much sense to anyone else? If you added an extensive key or a lengthy explanation of the model, someone else might be able to understand it, but that defeats the whole point of having a model.

In the 1980s, few hard and fast rules provided syntax for the creation of diagrams. By the middle of the 1990s, they were all fighting for supremacy (which was just as confusing). Today, the ubiquitous Unified Modeling Language (UML) defines the syntax of many forms of formal models.

Twenty years ago, standardized syntax was problematic for achieving unambiguous communication. Over time, the problem has been addressed and formal standardized grammars are now available for programs, diagrams, documents, and other kinds of communication. If a group is using the same syntax and grammar, we have solved at least part of our communication problem. As long as the Elephant Eater has a good grasp of formal grammars, it will be able to eat almost any form of standardized communication.

It's What You Say and When You Say It

If syntax is no longer a problem, then what about semantics and context? Even if groups can communicate with one another in formal structures or syntax, when they record the concept of "check," as in the earlier example, using a syntax, the word might not mean the same thing. In Figure 3.5, the project has an Elephant Eater, which has already consumed some information. The blocks represent concepts, and the lines are semantic relationships between them. The diagram should be read as a number of short subject-verb-object sentences, with the arrow showing the direction of the sentence. The following sentences could already be extracted from the Elephant Eater:

- Cover is a process step.
- Write is a process step.
- Check is a process step.
- Cover, then write.
- Write, then check.
- Check has an expiration date.
- Check has a value.

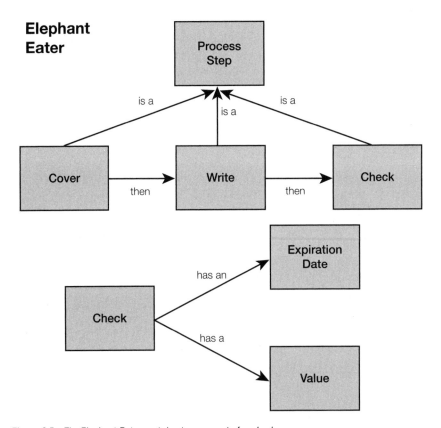

Figure 3.5 The Elephant Eater contains two concepts for *check*.

Apparently, we have some information about a simple process and some unrelated information about a financial check. Both pieces of information are separate, even though they share "check" as a concept.

Two more Views are now inserted into the Elephant Eater (see Figure 3.6). View A is from a process-modeling tool. View B is from a design model, which describes some of the core concepts for a retail bank computer program. Although the Views are in different formats, the Elephant Eater understands their syntax and can translate them into a similar form of simple sentences. View A can be read as follows:

- Check is a process step.
- Repeat is a process step.
- Check, then repeat.

View B would be read as follows:

- Check is an order of payment.
- Check has a value.

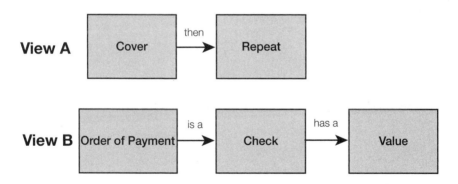

Figure 3.6 Two new Views need to be added to the information in the Elephant Eater—both Views contain the concept of "check."

Both Views contain the concept of "check," which makes the Views potentially ambiguous. The Elephant Eater can clarify this information in two ways. You can use the context of the Views to ensure that the information is inserted into the right area of the Elephant Eater. For example, "check" and "repeat" in View A are from a process-modeling tool, so as they are consumed by the Elephant Eater, they are both classed as process steps due to their context. After this is done, you realize that the information from View A can link to the existing process information stored in the Elephant Eater.

In the case of View B, the Elephant Eater would detect that "View B: Check" shares the same semantic relationship with "value" as one of the existing "check" instances in the Inventory. As a result, the Elephant Eater merges the information, as shown in Figure 3.7. The Elephant Eater now stores the facts that checks have values and expiration dates, but that they are also a kind of payment order.

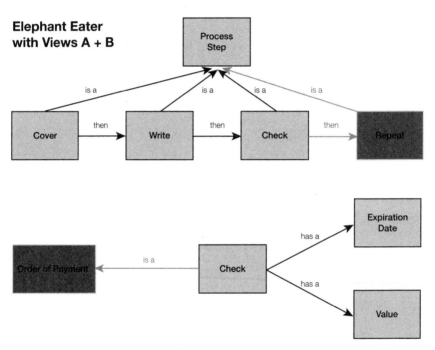

Figure 3.7   The Views have been successfully added to the Elephant Eater—semantics and context have been used to clarify the information.

Using this process to feed all the Views into the Elephant Eater, we can avoid project documentation ambiguity. The combination of syntax, semantics, and context provides a single source of truth, which we can use to understand the surrounding environment, the requirement, and, ultimately, the solution that is created. Inconsistency between Views is short lived because the Elephant Eater checks all new incoming information for consistency with the other information already contained inside.

This consistency checking also guards against parochialism. It is impossible to ignore the rest of the project if your perspective of it is checked daily against everyone else's.

Views aren't the only thing defining the solution that is fed into the Elephant Eater—the definitions of the environment that surrounds the solution contribute, too. In this way, it is possible to understand the environmental complexity and use it to ensure system compatibility.

This approach needs strong governance to ensure compliance, but it is exceptionally powerful at guarding against costly mistakes and late discoveries of requirements. This approach is central to the next two Brownfield Beliefs:

- Establish One Version of the Truth
- Embrace Complexity

We've reviewed complexity, ambiguity, inconsistency, and parochialism— now, what can we do about our industry's unavoidable language speciation? The Elephant Eater's ability to consume any language with a formal syntax means that language speciation is less of a problem. As long as a consistent translation exists between terms, you can express the Views in any language with a strong syntax. Indeed, the Brownfield approach actually recommends that Views be maintained in a native form selected by the maintainers and consumers of that View. This gives us our next Belief:

- Use Your Own Language

After the Views are unified, the amount of information inside the Elephant Eater becomes very large and complex. To ensure that we can successfully communicate this information to the business and project sponsors, we must make sure it is not too formal or technical. The instruction to "use your own language" flows both ways, not just in defining the information consumed by the Elephant Eater, but also in ensuring that any information issued from it is done in a suitable form for its consumer.

As you will see in the next chapter, Brownfield has much to offer in the area of communication, especially in bridging the communication gap between business and IT.

Architecting the Elephant Eater

We explained previously how the Elephant Eater consumes the complexity on a project. This approach enables people to continue using their own languages to define their Views while resolving inconsistencies and ambiguities, to ensure that the project stays on track. How is such an Elephant Eater constructed?

You could build such a beast in many ways, but IBM has built and patented its own version of an Elephant Eater using a tooling architecture called VITA, shown in Figure 3.8.

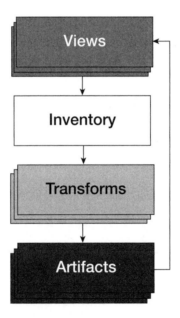

Figure 3.8   The Views, Inventory, Transforms, and Artifacts describe constituent parts of the Elephant Eater.

VITA is an acronym for Views, Inventory, Transforms, and Artifacts:

- Views describe the systems or processes that explain aspects of business or IT.
- Inventory is the repository that stores the information from the Views.
- Transforms define the relationships between concepts.
- Artifacts are the results generated from the Inventory.

The four elements fit together in an iterative process, which is the focus of the rest of this chapter.

Views

We introduced Views in the previous chapter as human perspectives of complex projects or systems. In the context of VITA, we need to define them more tightly. Views are formal[1] descriptions of systems or processes that enable business or IT goals to be met. The Views must be produced in a formal manner (using a syntax) so that users can interpret them in an unambiguous way, as described earlier. Views are typically maintained by one or a small group of individuals with similar concerns, so they usually correspond to the perspectives discussed in the last chapter.

Views are the outputs from your requirements capture, whether those requirements are functional or nonfunctional, or the constraints of your existing environments that we mentioned in Chapter 1, "Eating Elephants Is Difficult." Views can be static or dynamic in nature—that is, the concepts and relationships in the Views might be defined so that they have beginning and ending points in time. Therefore, it is possible for a View to describe either a single point in time or a whole series of different time periods.

Surprisingly, requirements often are captured with ambiguous methods, using tools that are designed to support normal office functions (such as word processing) instead of defining and designing new IT systems. The Brownfield approach encourages an end to such practices wherever possible, but it does not mandate that particular tools be used to capture these requirements and create these Views. Any tool that uses a consistent syntax to capture the information is sufficient. You can use Office tools, but they require a lot of discipline to ensure consistency. If they are the only option available to maintain Views, we have found spreadsheets to be more helpful than word processors.

The functional and nonfunctional requirements will normally be created specifically for the project. They are the business requirements of the real problem that you are trying to solve. In Brownfield, the specific method and tool is not as important as the capability to capture and output this information as a formal description. The use of the Unified Modeling Language is encouraged along with formal tools for defining business processes, the system design itself, and the data it needs to process. Users can treat each of these elements as separate Views using existing formal tooling.

In addition to the functional and nonfunctional requirements, a third type of requirement exists: constraints. These often are imported from the existing environment, but they might also be derived from artificial constraints driven by legislation, contracts, standards, strategies, or enterprise architecture requirements.

The descriptions of the existing environment likely will come from numerous sources, some of which might exist in a structured format. For example, interfaces might have formal definitions, and existing database structures are also likely to be defined and documented. However, many of these constraints might not be documented in any way, or that documentation might have been lost or not updated. In such cases, it might be possible to discover some of these constraints.

You can discover these constraints in two basic ways. The first is to use a manual iterative cycle of testing, discovering new requirements until you develop a more complete picture of the environment. The second is to use automated tools to discover these constraints. In recent years, a number of "static" program-analysis tools have been developed to analyze and document existing program code and database structures. You can feed the output of these tools into the Elephant Eater as a source of requirements (especially constraints). This trend for automated discovery will likely continue in the future.

Whether an iterative discovery cycle or static analysis is used to discover the existing environmental complexity, the result is a documented set of Views that contains many previously unknown or ignored constraining requirements.

Inventory

The Views described previously are collected and stored in a single repository called the Inventory. Views are imported into the Inventory via importers. IBM's Elephant Eater already has a large number of importers to translate many common types of Views. Users can easily build Importers as required to cope with new and different Views from different methods and tools.

The importers translate the Views into a common form within the Inventory. The Inventory must be kept consistent, so the importers check the View and ensure that it is consistent with the information that the Inventory already contains. As you learned when we clarified the check example earlier in the chapter, the importers check a number of rules to ensure that the View and information within the Inventory are consistent. If any inconsistencies or potential ambiguities are identified, these need to be corrected before the information can be imported.

For the importers to read in the Views and translate them into the Inventory, you would expect the Inventory to be extremely complex in structure. This couldn't be further from the truth: The Inventory is extremely simple and mimics how the human mind associates information. The method the Inventory uses to store and structure the information, called a triple, basically emulates how a baby would speak.

As you would suspect from the name, triples consist of three pieces of information: usually subject, verb, and object. You can use these triples to relate items in everyday life. "Player kicks ball" is a simple example of a triple. The subject is *player,* the verb is *to kick,* and the object is *ball.* Although this is an extremely simple construct, this method forms the basis of the Inventory, and we can use it to describe extremely complex relationships.

The power of the Inventory is its capability to eat almost any type of View and interlink the new information with its existing entries. As its knowledge of the existing environment and the new system grows, we can use it to supply information for increasingly sophisticated tasks.

Transforms

Many of these tasks are enabled by the Transform capability, which describes how concepts within the Inventory interrelate. In an ideal world, a business would handle a concept in one way. In reality, however, businesses end up with concepts being addressed in different ways in different parts of the business. For example, a person might be simultaneously an employee, a customer, and a manager. The information held about each of those types of person might be different, but there might be a single individual who is all of these things at once. In such circumstances, transformations are required to translate between the different ways in which a business represents the same thing. For example, it would be ideal for every system in a business to use and maintain exactly the same information for the same person and for any information held about the person, which was stored on more than one business system, to be consistent across all of them. Unfortunately, due to the division of businesses into departments or via the process of mergers and acquisitions, such a world rarely exists. In the world of Brownfield environments, the same data or concepts commonly are stored in many different formats in multiple systems while the enterprise has grown organically. As a result, transformations are needed to match up the way different systems handle the same concept.

To illustrate how a transformation shows the relationships between concepts, consider a very simple example in which customers' names are stored on two separate systems. On system A, the name is stored as a single field containing the full name. On system B, the name is stored in two separate fields, one for the family name and the second for the first name.

The fields are fundamentally storing the same data, but in slightly different ways. Transferring the name data requires a number of transformations to be defined. These transforms are dependent upon the direction in which the data is being transferred.

To transfer the name from system B to system A, a very simple transformation is required. System A requires the first name field and the family name field to be combined and separated by a single space.

Transferring the name from system A to system B requires two transformations. The first transformation to fill in the first name needs to extract all the names before the last space in the name in system B. The second transformation for the family name performs a similar process, but this time extracting the name after the last space.

Transforms enable the Elephant Eater not only to store basic concepts and their relationships, but also to store information about how these concepts interrelate. Such a transformation capability underpins many of the difficult and complex tasks we face on large projects, such as migrating data between systems and linking systems. To enable this to happen, the Elephant Eater uses its stored concepts, relationships, and Transforms to create Artifacts.

Artifacts

The concepts, relationships, and Transforms collected in the Inventory from multiple sources can help in a project only if we can use the Elephant Eater to inform and accelerate the production of the solution that is required. Instead of just being a repository of information, the Elephant Eater can be used to create a wide variety of Artifacts.

This capability of the Elephant Eater is based on an IT industry practice called Model Driven Development (MDD).[2] On a simple level, the approach enables code to be generated from the kinds of models we have been discussing instead of programmers writing them by hand. Our Brownfield approach similarly uses the information in the Inventory, along with the Transforms, to generate a wide variety of Artifacts. The term *artifact* is used to cover all outputs that the Inventory information can generate. Typically, these outputs include documentation, configuration, executables, and test cases.

Documents Should Be Generated Instead of Written

Documentation is probably the easiest type of Artifact to understand. The Inventory holds most information about an entire organization. Therefore, it is only natural that one of its uses is to produce documentation that describes this environment. This documentation should be in the language (or format) of the consumer. Although the Views were input in a formal way, the output can be a simple word-processed document.

You can use the Inventory to produce documentation at all levels, from high-level, system- or enterprise-level overviews down to detailed system documentation regarding a particular interface or database table. We look at how this is done in the next chapter.

The great power of this technique is that all the documentation is generated instead of written by hand. As a result, it is self-consistent, and references between artifacts are always current. By ensuring that the information is consistently fed into the Inventory, we ensure that any output documentation is also consistent—whatever form the documentation might take. The output is often diagrams, Microsoft Word documents, or spreadsheets—whatever is most suitable for the consumer of the information.

Consistent Configuration

Configuration artifacts are another category of output that the Inventory can generate. Configuration artifacts are used to define, set up, or control products within your IT estate. For many products, their configuration is stored in specially formatted text files that can be edited directly. Increasingly, the configuration files are generated as a result of user inputs. For example, most modern databases use standard formatted configuration files to define the database layout and structure. For many other products, proprietary configuration formats currently exist.

The use of MDD and the merging of information from many different Views into the Inventory enable the Elephant Eater to produce configuration artifacts for either standard or proprietary formats. This enables us to efficiently maintain database, package, and system configurations, and ensure consistency among them.

Efficient Execution

Executable artifacts are run within a computer system to perform a business task. Frequently, this is program code, but it can also include user interface screens, interface definitions, or rules for business rules engines. These Artifacts are generated from the information within the Inventory and can provide consistency across your enterprise. For example, a change to a concept in the Inventory might require changes to the user interface, the rules engine, and the database configuration. Fortunately, because these elements are now generated, ensuring consistency and verifying that all changes are made efficiently is no longer an issue.

Indeed, this capability to quickly make changes across a hugely complex system by changing one element of the requirement and watching that change result in the automatic regeneration of potentially hundreds of Artifacts shows how the Brownfield approach answers one of the problems raised in Chapter 1. In that chapter, we introduced the ripple effect, in which the interconnected complexity of a large environment can make small changes potentially costly and lengthy—the small change can create a ripple of changes, resulting in lengthy analysis, many manual changes, and massive retesting and reintegration. This is not the case with Brownfield. In our approach, the ripple is absorbed within the Inventory, and all the necessary changes to Artifacts are made when the solution is next generated. Admittedly, a change to a core concept (such as a customer) could result in huge numbers of Artifacts being changed and, thus, needing to be tested— but we have a mechanism to deal with that, too....

Testing Transforms

In addition to the documentation, configuration, and executables, the Elephant Eater can produce test artifacts. These test artifacts are designed to test the code that the Elephant Eater itself has generated.

It might seem strange to have the same system generate both the code to be tested and the tests to prove that code. However, a major part of everyday testing is to ensure that the system works as specified. The Inventory contains the information on all the constraints and valid values for the Artifacts that it produces, so the Inventory is in an excellent position to generate exhaustive test scripts and data to ensure that the requirements are all satisfied. Naturally, it uses a generation approach independent from the one that was used to generate the system itself.

With such a strong capability for test generation and self-testing, the Elephant Eater enables us to cope with ripple effects caused by environmental complexity. We can perform significant automated testing (regression testing) to ensure that the system still works as expected after an important change has rippled through the system.

When the automated Elephant Eater-based tests are complete, users and the system's operators must perform overall acceptance tests to ensure that what was fed into the Elephant Eater as the requirement actually satisfies the business and technical needs. Because Brownfield is an accelerated, iterative process, we can quickly incorporate new requirements discovered at either testing state and generate a new system.

The Elephant Eater in Action

The Views, Inventory, Transforms, and Artifacts that make up VITA are the core elements that make up the Elephant Eater. By feeding all requirements, including constraints, into a single place (the Inventory) and ensuring consistency among them, you maintain in the Inventory a single source of "truth" for your project. Thus, you gain an always-consistent solution.

On one $600 million government project, the system being developed used a heavily scripted user interface to capture information. This information was stored within the system until a number of interviews were completed and all the required information was captured. The information was then split and passed on to a number of legacy systems for processing. Unfortunately, the legacy systems were rejecting the messages because the information they received was incomplete.

The cause was simple: The rules used to generate the scripted questions and gather the information were not the same as the rules that the legacy systems used to validate that data. The two sides were generated from their own models, and those models didn't quite match. This wasn't as obvious a mistake as it would seem because more than 1,300 questions were used. The two parts of the solution were not completely consistent.

—K.J.

Figure 3.9 shows an example of an Elephant Eater in action. First, we decide which Views we need to support the project and solution. In this particular case, we identify that we need three Views. One provides a business perspective (including the frequencies of business transactions), another provides the logical design of the system, and the final View contains the infrastructure design. The initial harvesting of these three Views from existing sources and converting them into a standard syntax form is known as the site survey.

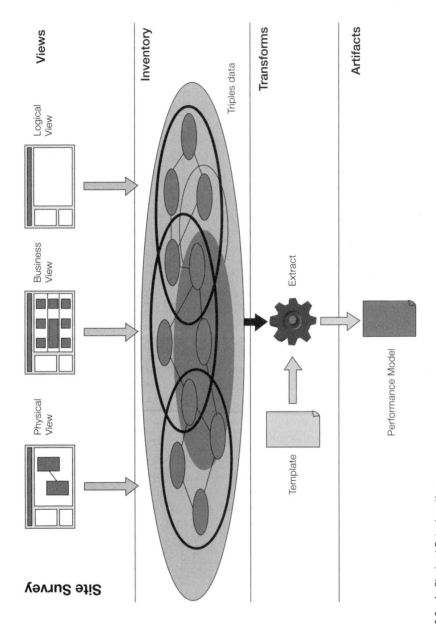

Figure 3.9 An Elephant Eater in action

In the example, these Views are fed into the Inventory from three separate tools. This is not unusual because each perspective is different and likely is maintained by a separate team. Each View provides a different perspective of the same solution. As they are imported into the Inventory, their contents are checked for consistency. The Inventory importers have been programmed with a number of simple rules that the system can use to check the consistency of the Inventory:

- Every component in the logical View must be located on a computer in the infrastructure View.
- Every computer in the infrastructure View must support at least one component.

After the Views are imported, they form a single interlinked body of knowledge expressed in triples. Regardless of how the information was fed in (shown by the three black outlined ovals), the system can produce a new extract of information from the Inventory that contains information from any or all of the original sources. In this case, the shaded extract uses some data from each of the Views.

This extract is used with any relevant Transforms and MDD techniques to generate a new Artifact. In this case, the elements are combined to automatically generate a performance model that predicts how big the hardware elements for this new system need to be and how long it will take to process each business transaction. The same extract can be used to generate many other Artifacts.

The great beauty of this approach is that as the Views change, the performance model changes with them. We can quickly and confidently predict the hardware cost of a business or system design change instead of manually impacting the change and trying to keep the performance model in step with three rapidly changing Views. Design optimization and priority balancing becomes much easier and is achieved in a dynamic and iterative way.

The Brownfield Lifecycle

Figure 3.9 showed how a Brownfield project is built using Views as input to create a "single source of truth" in the Inventory. Of course, this is not necessarily the complete truth, nor is it necessarily true. The Inventory is just a well-documented collection of the requirements (Views), neatly cross-referenced. It is effectively a baseline understanding of the project at that point in time. The Inventory might be consistent and unambiguous, but the Views that populate it could still be wrong or incomplete. This is why Brownfield puts such an emphasis on early testing.

The Brownfield approach differs from the Greenfield approach, in that the nature of processing the requirement does not change during the lifecycle—however late a defect is discovered. In Greenfield approaches, the focus of defect fixing and testing moves from high-level design, to low-level design, to code, and then back out again through a variety of testing phases. Brownfield development ensures that the requirement is always maintained, not the end product. Every iteration brings you closer to your complete set of requirements and the solution. Figure 3.10 describes this lifecycle.

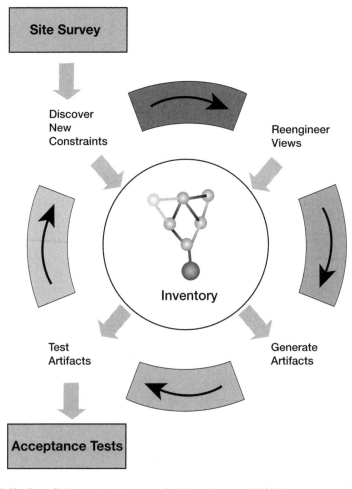

Figure 3.10   Brownfield is an iterative approach designed to cope with highly complex situations.

The lifecycle starts with a site survey, as described earlier, and then moves into an iterative development and testing cycle. Within that cycle, we iteratively do the following:

1. **Discover further information about the problem by feeding in information from existing sources**—Sometimes converting the existing information into a formal View suitable for the Inventory can take significant effort, and often it is most effective to feed in the information in stages.

2. **Reengineer the information in the Views to reflect our latest understanding of the requirements**—Artifacts are always regenerated instead of edited directly, so editing the Views (often expressed as UML models during re-engineering) or the patterns that are used to define the Artifacts is the way we create the solution. We use this method to correct any defects that the Inventory import process identifies.

3. **Regenerate the Artifacts**—You should do this on a regular basis so that people know when Views need to reach a point of consistency. Each time, the Views are imported into the Inventory and the system produces a list of import errors for correction.

4. **Test the Artifacts**—The configuration and executable Artifacts are automatically tested to ensure that the Inventory definition and the behavior of the executing components match. The system feeds defects back to the View owners for correction.

The iterative and generation aspects of Brownfield are important, so we give them a Brownfield Belief of their own.

Iteratively Generate and Refine

When the Elephant Eater is in place, it changes the whole way we can efficiently execute projects. We can now generate a large proportion of the solution on a regular basis instead of writing it by hand. In addition, the generated elements are kept in step with the Inventory, and each other, with minimal effort. Indeed, on a Brownfield project, we would expect to see all artifacts regenerated on a daily (or nightly) basis.

This enforced consistency of requirements provides a robust, yet highly adaptable platform on which to build large and complex solutions. As the Inventory changes, the generated Artifacts also change with minimal effort. As a result, an initial import of information into the Inventory from a site survey might be enough to begin generating and testing elements of the solution much earlier in a project lifecycle than was previously possible. As you saw in Chapter 1, early defect detection is a highly advantageous strategy. The Brownfield approach makes it possible to quickly build solutions, test them against the real environment, find out where the requirements are lacking or poorly defined, and fix them. Because the solution is built up incrementally on firm foundations, this is a cost-effective and superb way of handling both system and environmental complexity.

Brownfield is designed to work alongside existing environments. The site survey is not just a way of feeding in environmental complexity; it is also a way of absorbing that complexity to reengineer and incrementally change it. Brownfield is not about throwing away existing systems, but instead enabling them to be reengineered piece by piece in a controlled manner. The use of discovery techniques in the site survey and the capability to "eat" existing complexity leads us to the last of our Brownfield Beliefs....

Use What's Around

Brownfield opens up the possibility of incremental change and greater reuse of existing systems to deliver new solutions in complex environments.

The Brownfield Beliefs

The Brownfield Beliefs represent a new way of thinking about delivering complex systems instead of a set of technologies or products. To change something so fundamental, you need an easily communicable set of ideas instead of 200 pages of prose. Therefore, the Brownfield Beliefs form the blueprints of the Elephant Eater, as shown in Figure 3.11.

Now that we've introduced them individually, we can consolidate them in one place. The Brownfield Beliefs are:

- Make Business and IT Indivisible
- Establish One Version of the Truth
- Embrace Complexity
- Use Your Own Language
- Iteratively Generate and Refine
- Use What's Around

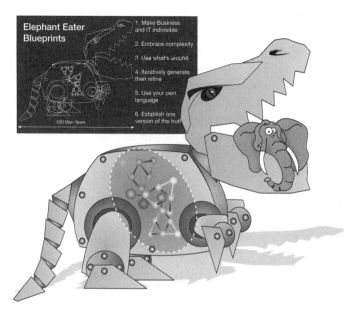

Figure 3.11 We designed the Elephant Eater in line with the Brownfield Beliefs.

Many of these beliefs have a strong technical aspect to them, so although this chapter provides an overview of what they mean and why they are important, each one is covered in more detail in Part II, "The Elephant Eater." The rest of this chapter summarizes the beliefs, and points the reader in the direction of further information, if desired.

Make Business and IT Indivisible

IT is rarely a means to its own end. The move toward SOA is drawing IT and business closer than they have been for many years. Even so, many businesses still have separate groups within the IT organization fashioning the service requirements, and another group designing and deploying the solution.

Business and IT are intrinsically linked. A change in one ripples through to the other. Business and IT need to get used to this idea and start dealing with it properly. Changing an aspect of the business should be understood in the context of an IT change, and vice versa. Maintaining such traceability between the two domains as a matter of course is currently rare. We return to this theme in the next chapter to see how Brownfield meets this need.

Embrace Complexity

Assuming that the world can be simplified is an assumption that appears to underpin the fundamental nature of the IT industry. Poor technical assumptions (generalizations and abstractions) during the early stages of projects—when the genuine complexity of the surrounding environment and the solution tends to be conveniently ignored—give projects a false sense of security. Using traditional Greenfield techniques, the IT industry sets out to build on very complex Brownfield sites by ignoring hundreds or thousands of relevant constraints until it is too late—or simply very expensive to cope with them.

Chaos theory tells us that even the simplest systems can be unpredictable. Humans, businesses, and economies are not simple, and change can be chaotic with multiple feedback loops and ripple effects.

The IT industry and business need to recognize the complexity of reality instead of taking a sanitized, generalized, and poorly abstracted "fluffy cloud" view of the world. To do this efficiently, we need to find automated ways of discovering what is out there and recording its complexity. We further elaborate on this belief in Chapter 6, "Abstraction Works Only in a Perfect World."

Use What's Around

Solutions for Brownfield sites must be cost-effective and optimizable, because the cost of maintaining the Brownfield itself absorbs a significant portion of the IT budget. Writing thousands of lines of code by hand is no longer an effective, maintainable, or acceptable, answer. Packages, software reuse, and legacy reuse need to be part of the solution, not part of the problem.

After the Elephant Eater discovers the complexity of Brownfield sites, it becomes possible to find effective ways of working with them and changing them incrementally. Strategies include incorporating packages, reusing existing code, and using MDD. We can even start using the power of the VITA architecture to perform software archeology on the legacy systems. By feeding legacy code and configuration files into the Elephant Eater as part of the site survey, we can mine and communicate the lost structures and patterns of the legacy code in new ways. In this way, we can begin to rebuild the legacy systems according to new patterns and technologies. Applications generated from the Inventory and comprised of components from many sources become the norm instead of the exception.

We explain how this software archeology is performed using the Elephant Eater in Chapter 9, "Inside the Elephant Eater."

Iteratively Generate and Refine

Adopting these approaches means that we can iteratively refine and test complex areas such as interface behavior or legacy business rules, similar to how agile development techniques changed the way the IT industry defines user interfaces (via direct interaction with the real world instead of the creation of theoretical specifications in isolation).

These innovations, combined with intelligent new ways of working with the existing Brownfield sites, result in smaller projects with a faster turnaround and greater levels of reuse. Projects become more incremental than revolutionary, reducing their overall risk and gradually reducing the maintenance cost. Chapter 8, "Brownfield Development," elaborates on this topic.

Use Your Own Language

Feeding information into the Elephant Eater can't be done in some complex and precise dialect that everyone needs to learn. Just as Brownfield embraces complexity, it also embraces the idea that people genuinely need to look at problems in different ways and use different vocabularies. They need to speak their own language and create and maintain their own Views.

It is also imperative that the Elephant Eater communicates and relates the relevant information that it has digested so that we can build a new solution. Detail is often a necessary and desirable part of that communication, especially when generating code or configurations; however, summaries are also necessary to ensure that the Elephant Eater can communicate high-level information to people who don't want to see the detail. These more abstract perspectives are created from the detail in the Inventory. Therefore, these perspectives are more reliable than the high-level information that IT architects using conventional Greenfield techniques often create and issue.

These outward communications from the Elephant Eater (the Artifacts) must be in multiple recognized languages (computer code, English, design languages or models, and so on) and multiple forms (text files, Microsoft Word, pictures, and so on) while maintaining the formal and precise meaning.

Ideally, the Elephant Eater will be such a good communicator that informal communication tools, such as PowerPoint or Visio, could be eliminated in most cases. We cover this topic in Chapter 4, "The Trunk Road to the Brain."

Establish One Version of the Truth

However, for the Elephant Eater to work, each of those native format Views must be hooked into a single conceptual body of knowledge defining the overall environment and solution.

Ambiguity and inconsistencies are removed incrementally by converting imprecise documents to precise Views. These Views are combined in the Inventory, and then inconsistencies, ambiguities, and missing information are incrementally identified and corrected. In this way, natural language-based ambiguities—that is, Word or natural English-based specifications and designs—are gradually excised from the definition of the requirement. The requirement and, ultimately, the solution design become defined by the consistent and formal combination of all the Views. Ultimately, a recognizable and comprehensive single version of the truth emerges, to describe the whole of the environment and the solution expressed in terms of multiple, combined Views within the Inventory. This definition can then be used to generate much or all of the solution.

Bridging the Business/IT Gap

These Brownfield Beliefs set the bar very high for a new way of working. But as the first two chapters explained, some fundamental areas of the IT industry's approach need to change if the delivery of complex change into complex environments is to become a repeatable and predictable process that does not rely upon big-mouthed superheroes.

In the next chapter, we look at how we can complement this capability to build complex systems in complex Brownfield IT environments with another Brownfield unique capability: new communication mechanisms to help bridge the communication gap between business and IT.

Endnotes

1   Strictly speaking, most of the methods used are described as semiformal, because formal methods use mathematically based techniques to define your solution. Such techniques are normally used only when safety or security is seen as critical.

2   MDD is a software engineering approach launched by the Object Management Group standards consortium.

4

The Trunk Road
to the Brain

"If the dull substance of my flesh were thought,
Injurious distance should not stop my way;
For then, despite of space, I would be brought
From limits far remote where thou dost stay
No matter then although my foot did stand
Upon the farthest earth removed from thee,
For nimble thought can jump both sea and land
As soon as think the place where he would be."

William Shakespeare, Sonnet 44

Chapter Contents

- Alternative Wallpapers   66
- Invading Hilbert Space   72
- Architecture Is the Solution   75
- Bridging the Business/IT Gap   79

The previous chapter introduced how Brownfield unites information in the Inventory. In this chapter, we show how combining formal Views that span business and IT results in a unique capability to create new levels of cooperation between the domains.

This chapter shows that recording the business and IT information in the kinds of Views introduced in the last chapter makes it possible for both business and IT professionals to reach a common understanding of the requirement and the solution.

This level of traceability and linkage between the requirement and the solution is generally associated with extremely heavyweight systems engineering methods. This chapter shows that such traceability and combined understanding of both business requirements and IT solutions is possible within a lightweight and fast agile development process.

The Brownfield approach lends itself to the creation of uniquely powerful perspectives that provide a new level of understanding between business and IT. We examine this perspective, which exploits the highway (or trunk road, if you know the equivalent UK term and want to extend the Elephant analogy a little further) to the brain, in this chapter.

Alternative Wallpapers

As we have already discussed, the greatest source of IT project failure is not technology, but communication of complexity. Therefore, you might rightly expect that optimizing communication receives a great deal of attention. You might assume that the architects and technicians will do everything possible to ensure that the business understands their design and to provide a useful and full explanation of the problem. Surprisingly, however, achieving this level of communication with the business is rarely a priority.

Except for use cases, which usually create a good bridge between IT formality and business English, the IT industry has precious few other examples to be proud of.

Use cases combine standard English and some simple rules that cover their formatting and level of detail to ensure that both the business and the IT personnel can understand the requirement. However, Chapter 2, "The Confusion of Tongues," showed that the English language is a poor medium for precise communication. In addition, language is one of the least direct ways of getting information into the brain. The immediate senses of seeing, hearing, touching, and smelling have far more immediate routes in. Many memory techniques work by converting information into visual scenes or mini mental plays, to make complex information much more memorable. In the IT industry, our ability to exploit these other routes, especially the visual cortex to achieve communication, is woeful.

To ensure that we have a good formal definition of our design processes, the IT industry loves to dream up new formal ways of portraying them. As we saw in Chapter 2, many of the improvements in communication in the IT industry have come down to a formalization of syntax (the structure of the language), which removes some structural ambiguity. The downside of such innovation is the creation of highly formal, structured, and private languages. Unless you've been trained in them, your chances of understanding them are slim—even when they are simple line drawings.

On one of our previous projects, the "best" communication mechanism was to create business process definitions. To ensure buy-in, these processes were stuck up on the wall so that people could become familiar with them and consult them whenever they wanted. The processes were created according to a semiformal specification in a drawing tool so that everyone could work on them.

Conventionally, we generally did such diagrams vertically in a formal tool and collated them into documents or websites for publication purposes. However, the instruction to paste them on the wall required that they be printed horizontally—there simply weren't enough stairwells in the building.

Now, although this decision might have been very sensible for a small project, this was one of the elephantine projects we're talking about.

As a result, every wall on the program became covered with process flows. Many flowed all the way around rather substantial rooms. At the end of the process, we had some very long, pretty pictures, but little formal understanding of the whole process and how it linked.

The scale of the pictures was horrifying. Seeing all this complexity at one glance (albeit, in one rather long sideways glance) scared people. Instead of feeling more comfortable with the complexity, people were disturbed by it.

In addition, using these pictures for anything formal would have been impossible. The team that created them had created a private semiformal language that was not quite formal enough for the design team to use directly, but too formal for the business to readily understand.

—R.H. and K.J.

Such gaps in communication can be extremely costly. The "experiment" in communication in the previous anecdote (which had worked okay on smaller projects with less direct user involvement) was identified as a mistake. These diagrams needed to be translated into a formal tool so they could be maintained, tracked, and refined until they were useful. Unfortunately, the problems that the informal documents had created had already undermined customer confidence in the project as a whole—the project closed down at a huge cost.

Formal communication can be just as ineffective as informal communication, however. The use of formal representations with formal syntaxes such as UML, RDF/OWL, DDL, BNF, and a host of other three-letter acronyms can be even scarier for the uninitiated.

In addition, the amount of information that can be packed into these tools is worrying. Anyone who has worked on a big project will remember fondly the huge ANSI E-sized or A0-sized diagram that almost every such project has stuck to a prominent wall or notice board. Whether it's the Component Model, which describes the internal structure of what is being built; or the Logical Data Model, which describes the data structures the system has to deal with; or a detailed Infrastructure diagram, they all have the power to terrify through complexity. In many projects, we have seen the architect or designer in charge finally manage to download the drivers for a particularly big plotter or printer, and then take great delight in printing out his or her masterpiece so that everyone could finally read the small print. Figure 4.1 caricatures this tendency of lead technical personnel to blind everyone else with science.

On the same project that involves walls papered by process flows, one of the lead architects was famous for answering any question about the system by presenting a slide extracted from the project's similarly gargantuan Component Model. It did not matter if the question was about the user interface, the physical infrastructure supporting the system, or a detail in the business process. Of course, despite its size, the Component Model contained absolutely no useful information with regard to these topics. But this didn't matter. With an astonishing ability to blind with science, the architect explained the answer in the context of a language that the architect was particularly happy with and the audience had little or no knowledge of. Almost always, they went away slightly confused but basically happy, much to the amusement of every other architect in the room.

The barrier in communication that the private language created was, in this case, of some benefit to the architect—but, fortunately, the project was canceled before the joke wore too thin.

—R.H.

Figure 4.1 An architect describes each box on his diagram that provides a high-level perspective of the whole of the system, much to the consternation of his audience.

The IT industry is quite happy to try to impose its own languages on the business. IT professionals often have sufficient hubris to believe: "They must conform to us, because we are precise and right." The science fiction writer Robert Heinlein understood the foolishness of this attitude and expressed it in a famous quote illustrated in Figure 4.2. If the IT industry thought hard about it, it would realize that the privately formatted diagrams with hidden meanings are an exceptionally poor way to communicate anything outside of the IT domain.

Figure 4.2   "Never try to teach a pig to sing. It wastes your time and annoys the pig." (Robert Heinlein, *Time Enough for Love.* Ace, 1987)

This kind of experience is painful for everyone involved. So how do we actually manage to communicate these complex concepts and difficult information on projects? The answer is both universal and appallingly simple.

We use PowerPoint.

Oh, yes! The universal tool for communicating any complex concept is to use PowerPoint. Of course, this tends to be a lot of work. Clearly, you can't just paste the complex information directly into a presentation and expect someone to follow it just because it's now on a slide. No, you have to lose all that precision and formality that you've just spent a lot of time creating for your downstream consumers (the designers or the coders or the testers) and informally abstract it to the level of your audience.

If you're following a formal method, you will probably have some inter-mediate summary- or architecture-level materials that will pad out your presentation and guide the listener to the right area. But to get the approval you're seeking, chances are, you have to create a new level of abstraction to convey the complex and detailed concept you're looking at.

If you're lucky, this could be a diagram you can draw from the existing information you have in your design tool. (Rational® enables you to do this with UML diagrams, for example.) More often, though, such automated out-puts retain the frightening aspects of the private language they were written in. This might include a lot of punctuation where your English teacher clearly told you it shouldn't go (<>I_();) or loads of odd abbreviations or EnglishWordsStuckTogether like a version of Anglo-Deutsch that has a problem with the capital Shift key. You might have to bite the bullet and create the ultimate in dangerous project dead-ends: the pretty-picture PowerPoint communication deck.

Such decks are dead ends for a variety of reasons:

- They are long and laborious to create in the first place.
- They are likely inaccurate, incomplete, or, at best, imprecise abstractions of the truth.
- The missing information makes them highly subjective (often one per-son's view of how everything works). The hilltop or view used by one writer might be confusing or might omit key details that a consumer or fellow presenter needs. When multiple people from different perspectives (such as process and organization) prepare such decks, they're almost always guaranteed to be inconsistent and to cause confusion in the audience.

Sadly, despite all this effort, nearly every presentation turns up someone in the audience who asks a question that requires referring to information that has been deliberately left out of the slides to make them easy to understand. Such are the dangers of trying to predict other people's Views. After pointing out such discrepancies and inadequacies of the presentation, how many pre-sentations have you attended at which the audience loses faith with the pre-senter or simply thinks, "You simply don't understand this"?

Even if the communication at the initial presentation works and the audi-ence walks away with copies of the presentation, what happens if they point out an inaccuracy during the presentation? Typically, the defect is captured in the room and the source data is updated with the new information—but will the presenter update the PowerPoint slides, too?

What happens if the original design or requirement materials change? Will the slide deck be changed then? Will it get reissued to everyone who attended the session?

Experience suggests that this won't be the case unless the presenter has to use the slides again fairly soon.

As a result, the hundreds of pages of PowerPoint will begin to diverge from the source data. Pretty soon they will be effectively worthless. However, because the audience has often walked away with a copy of the presentation, those pages can quickly become superb sources of confusion. If you're really unlucky, they might become a formal part of the baseline that you are asked to deliver to and will become a real millstone around your neck.

So how can an Elephant Eater communicate precisely without resorting to blinding science?

Invading Hilbert Space

The previous chapter introduced the Elephant Eater, which absorbs details from the surrounding environment using formal Views. Each of these Views represents a particular viewpoint of the problem space being examined.

Of course, this massively holistic process has a drawback. Although each individual View is easy to maintain and understand, the combined Inventory is massively complex. Now, this should not be overly surprising. By definition, the Inventory consists of a lot of combined perspectives—only a super-hero or an Elephant Eater could understand that complexity. A highly precise and high-capacity computer might be capable of storing and processing the Inventory as a whole, but no human could easily cram the combined information into his or her head.

If we did try to display the Inventory as a whole, it would be unimaginably complex. Imagine that each one of those short sentences that we called triples were drawn in two dimensions. The subject and object could be represented as a shape, such as a circle, and the relationship between them could be represented as a linking arrow (see Figure 4.3).

Now imagine an Inventory with thousands of such interrelated triples. The picture would not be dissimilar to Figure 4.1, but it would contain many more boxes and lines. If we tried to display the Inventory in two dimensions, lines would crisscross the paper like spaghetti. The time dimension of the Inventory also would mean that we might need a lot of copies to represent different time periods.

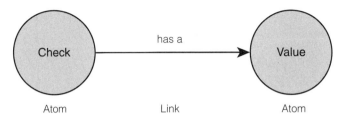

Figure 4.3 Each triple could be represented by a simple structure of atoms and links.

Each triple can have its own lifetime defined, so the number of these different time periods (often called time slices) could be very high. Three dimensions might provide a better representational space because different layers of the diagram could be used for different information, but the time dimension would require multiple copies of the three-dimensional model. If we wanted to see the whole Inventory in a single glance, we would probably have to use a multidimensional space with far more dimensions that we are used to exploring—more than the usual three plus time. We have something of a problem. Our Elephant Eater is actually a multidimensional monster of unimaginable complexity, impossible to visualize. Unfortunately, people don't like dealing with things that they can't see or understand. Lack of understanding breeds fear and lack of acceptance. We need to do something creative.

We have two problems here: one of too much information and one of how to represent complex interlinked data. If you had a lot of money to spend and a lot of time, you might decide to draw something by hand. But the more complex the graphic, the harder it is to maintain. Such an approach is another dead end because the Inventory changes daily; the picture could never keep up.

Manually Exploring the Inventory

Perhaps there's a way to present the Inventory so that it can be visualized and navigated?

One form of navigation would enable one subset of the Inventory to be seen at a time. The entire space could be explored by following the links between the atoms, as shown in Figure 4.4.

Fortunately, such tools do exist.[1,2] Many allow Inventory type data to be imported and then explored in this kind of dynamic way. The exploration can start at any particular atom. As atoms are selected, the surrounding data changes to depict the information surrounding that atom.

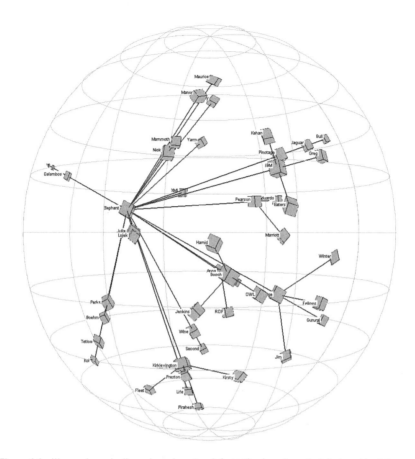

Figure 4.4 We can dynamically navigate Inventory information by using a tool designed to plot relationships. It's quirky and neat, but it could be more user friendly and isn't really suitable for a business audience.

Navigating the Inventory in this way makes it possible to ask and answer simple queries. Does this solve our concern about a lack of understanding of the Inventory? Maybe, but it might be hard to find the information that we want if we don't know where it is in the hierarchy. Plus, this isn't the most intuitive representation. A designer or developer might feel at home, but that's probably about it.

Alternatively, some tools even enable you to ask simple English-like questions about an Inventory. Such query languages, such as SPARQL, are relatively new but underline some of the power of the Inventory. Of course, because these semantically rich databases are relatively new, the tools that support them tend to be from research or early products—they are often not that user friendly, and their output is not easily understood.

Perhaps reading the Inventory directly is part of the problem. Might another way exist?

Architecture Is the Solution

For once in this book, perhaps architecture *is* part of the solution. This time, however, we're talking about building architecture, not the IT variety.

Fundamentally, building architects do things rather better than IT architects. Perhaps it's because they've had several centuries' head start, but whatever the reason, we should learn from them. For a building of any degree of complexity, architects tend to use Computer Aided Design (CAD) packages to put the building together. The various different layers of the building are available to peruse and can be displayed or hidden at will. Building architects know all about Views.

These CAD programs can output Artifacts specifically used for communication. Some Artifacts are traditional communications, such as blueprints and orthogonal Views. Sometimes the models are extracted as a different Artifact and reimported as a View into another tool that can turn the model into a full-color, three-dimensional representation augmented with trees, flowers, skies, and realistic materials.

Guided tours around the building can be given before the design is even approved—and, certainly, well before a single brick is laid or a girder is cast.

The lesson to take from this is that visualization and View maintenance and creation should be separate but automatically linked. The Views that are suitable for the building architect in designing and maintaining the design of a building are not suitable for showing to the client. The visualization Artifact that is used to give the client a guided tour would not work successfully as a View for designing the building. Having a Best of Breed in both areas in a single tool would be highly unusual. After all, this was one of the reasons that Brownfield supported multiple Views in the first place—no single optimal tool exists for maintaining all Views.

Note also that the marvelous odd-shaped buildings that today's architects revel in often can't be made physical without computers. The shapes that architects define within their CAD program are usually transferred to other programs so that they can be manufactured. Each strut and girder these days can be different and custom built. This technique, called Computer Aided Manufacturing (CAM), isn't new. Somewhat surprisingly, the computer industry equivalent, Computer Aided Software Engineering (CASE), never really took off. Only relatively recently has the Model Driven Architecture movement rekindled the interest in building software directly from models. We discuss why this is the case in Chapter 7, "Evolution of the Elephant Eater."

Ideally, we want a similar walkthrough of our Brownfield site and our new systems. If the CAD program can export to a 3D graphical rendering engine, why can't we? Why can't we export the Inventory data and visualize it?

Elephants Have Two Lives

Moving from today's static two-dimensional representations to a dynamic three-dimensional space would give us two opportunities. First, we could represent more interlinked data in an understandable way because we would have an extra dimension to play with. Most systems are multilayered these days, so this seems a pretty sensible way to go. In addition, if the space we're working in is dynamic, maybe we could show the dynamic nature of the problem and the solution. If we're showing a process, perhaps we could show the effects of that process as it flows. If we're showing a time series of Views, perhaps we could see them evolve. Furthermore, instead of using rather flat boxes and lines, perhaps each type of thing held in the Inventory could be given a different visual metaphor. We could then see how all these different types of things work together without needing to read all those labels and strange symbols. We'd be able to exploit the visual cortex, the highest-bandwidth route to the brain—the trunk road, no less.

Historically, such ideas have been expensive and difficult to achieve. For a fast three-dimensional display, you needed a dedicated and expensive CAD workstation. Even on expensive equipment, the rendering of a 3D walkthrough of a complex design could take many hours. In the last ten years, however, all that has changed. Even handheld computers can now process complex three-dimensional graphics in real time. As a result, feeding in complex information for real-time, three-dimensional animated visualization is pretty feasible. So we could do it that way, but why stop there?

One of the key problems we have continually identified in this book is communication. If we want to visualize our Inventory, why don't we do it so that the understanding can be shared rather than experienced by one person alone? And with the IT industry being increasingly global, perhaps we could do it in a way to share the understanding around the globe, in real time.

Such thoughts would have been close to insane even a couple years ago. At the time of this writing, however, millions of people have logged on and tried virtual worlds. In a generation or less, surely their use will be ubiquitous. Other than for playing games, many have wondered about possible uses for virtual worlds—others think it's the start of a 3D Internet.

These worlds provide the opportunity to share precise, three-dimensional, dynamic representations of information. You can also see other people interacting with the same information. If you know this information well, you could answer questions about it and share your understanding anywhere on the planet.

When this thought first occurred to us, the obvious choice of platform was Second Life, as shown in Figure 4.5.[3]

Figure 4.5 Second Life is a 3D virtual world environment with more than eight million individuals enrolled. Everything there is built by its users; this bridge and plaza is on IBM 1 and was built by one of the authors.

Second Life is an environment built entirely by the people who use it to meet and communicate. Second Life is not a game, but it has achieved world fame as a virtual world that is open for business. The difficulty of rendering Inventories in environments such as Second Life is twofold. First, the virtual world itself has no capability to store complex data, so the Inventory needs to be read in from outside the world. This can be solved by building a suitable interface.

The second is trickier. The Inventory has no "positional" data within it—the display algorithms must determine the shape the Inventory is displayed as. It's as if you've been given a long list of Metro or Tube stations along with some track information that tells you which ones are connected to each other. Unfortunately, you've been given no information about where the stations actually are, and you've been asked to work out the best way to lay out the map. Now, this is a complex task, so it could be performed outside of the virtual world. However, this would result in Inventories that would essentially be static in the virtual world, which seems a poor use of a highly dynamic environment. The solution was to make the displays self-organizing. Figure 4.6 shows an early model.

Figure 4.6 As the morning sun dawns on a new age in the IT industry, one of the authors (or, at least, his avatar) sits astride an early semantic model of an Inventory consisting of atoms and links.

This visualization shows a small part of the structure of a number of interfaces that are shared between three systems down to the attribute[4] level. Essentially, it is a single Inventory created by combining three overlapping Views. The atom and link structure of the Inventory is clearly visible.

Such visualizations are just the start, however.

Bridging the Business/IT Gap

Just as the Inventory can absorb technical information such as data models, component models, infrastructure, and interface models, it can also import business processes, use case models,[5] and classified business terms.[6] These kinds of information provide a user- and business-oriented perspective rather than technology-based perspective of the problem.

Formally linking this business information to the definition of the IT system within the Inventory makes it possible to start sophisticated analysis such as impact assessments. For example, if part of the system changes, we can use traceability between the business and IT spaces to understand which use cases should be retested. Alternatively, if a use case is significantly revised or dropped from the requirement, it is possible to analyze which areas of the system could be affected.

In recent years, tools have been created that define business processes in such a way that the information the tools hold can be exported for execution on a business process engine. We can use the same exports to import this dynamic perspective to the Inventory. The business processes thus defined enable us to link to other key business concerns, such as business data entities and resources (such as time, money, locations, and people).

Use cases are often identified within the business process as the boundary points between the primary and secondary actors (typically, the supporting systems). The full definition of these boundaries (along with the interface specifications) creates the systems context.

Formal use case data also often includes data entity manipulation data, such as which process updates which bit of business data. This information can form a bridge between the static logical data model and the dynamic business processes. This enables the Inventory to know what processes act on which data. Even if the use cases themselves are not sufficiently detailed to do this, the architects can create a process/data usage spreadsheet or database and use it to import the same data.

So if we can import all this business metadata,[7] IT metadata, and, most importantly, metadata that bridges the two perspectives as Views into the Inventory, can we build a visualization that provides new insight that traditional methods could never provide?

Figure 4.7 shows the conventional View of a combined business/IT picture that has been derived from a number of separate Views. To make the comparison that follows fair, we have used the autolayout feature of the tool to format the data for viewing.

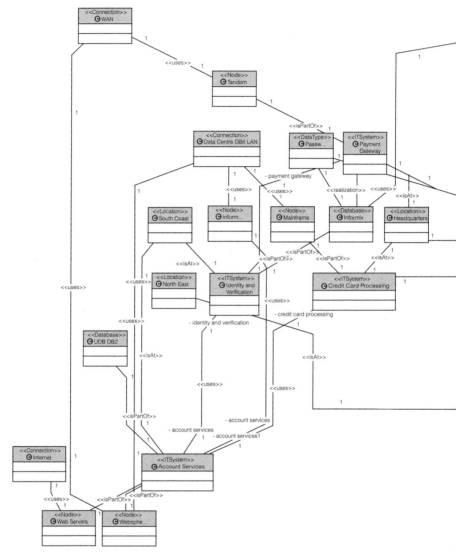

Figure 4.7 Even a small Inventory visualized in two dimensions using a UML tool is pretty hard to read.

It's not wonderfully clear or intuitive, is it? Explaining this perspective in its entirety to a business end user would require one of those marathon PowerPoint decks. Although the Inventory would still offer significant benefit in terms of traceability and impact analysis, in its current form, the merged model would not improve communication.

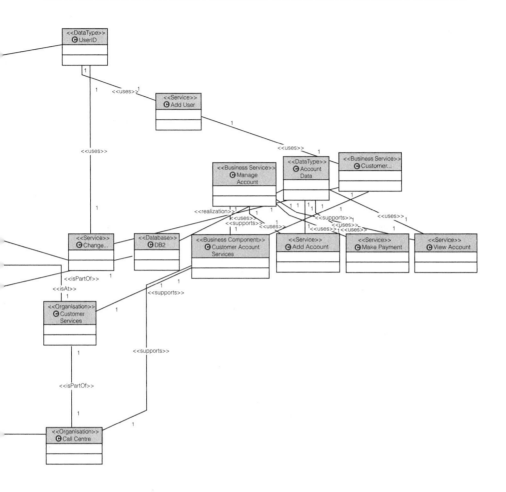

A better approach would be to translate this model into a three-dimensional layered picture.

Hidden within the morass of detail in Figure 4.7 are some implied layers, which we can see if we create a model of our model (that is, a metamodel). In this form (Figure 4.8), we can see the hidden structure of the data we were looking at.

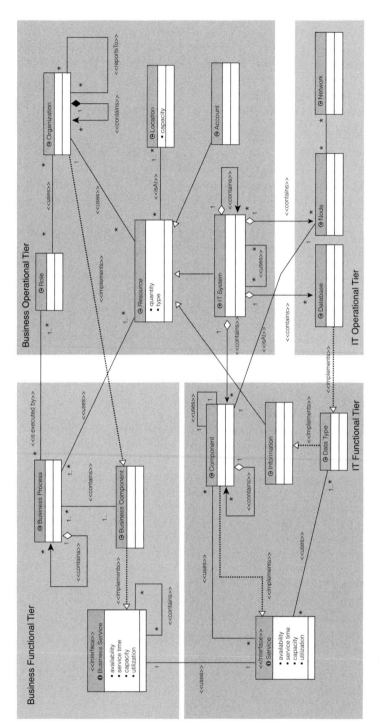

Figure 4.8 Even the model that describes the model is pretty confusing, but it provides a sense of structure by which we can begin to visualize the data.

The data is organized into a number of different areas, as indicated by the shaded rectangles behind them. The top-left part of the diagram describes the business services, which are the capabilities provided by processes that the business executes. (There is no IT in this view.) These business services are underpinned by the business itself, which has a set of resources that it uses to deliver these business functions. Some of these resources are IT systems, but locations, people, and money all play their part.

The IT systems are underpinned by physical structures, shown in the bottom right (computers, networks, and the like), and logical structures, in the bottom left (data, components, and interfaces). Finally, the IT systems provide IT services (bottom, far left), which support the business services (returning to the top left, where we started the description).

This is a pretty powerful vocabulary—it's not complete, by any means, but it gives a strong representation of the business-significant aspects of today's business and IT systems. It is not a business View or an IT View—it is both.

We can use this implied structure to create a similarly layered three-dimensional representation of the original complex data, as shown in Figure 4.9.

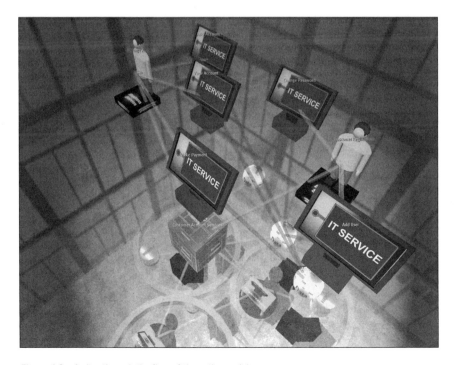

Figure 4.9 A view through the floor of the entire model

The Grand Tour

You can visit the model yourself on the IBM islands in Second Life (at Second Life grid reference [IBM 1 140, 150, 60] or http://slurl.com/secondlife/IBM%201/140/150/60). Each of the tiers represents the perspectives (sometimes combined perspectives) of one or more sets of users.

Figure 4.9 shows this whole model. You can clearly see the layers and linkages between them, but the eagle-eyed might notice that three-dimensional metaphors have replaced the atoms and links of the earlier representations.

Perhaps only the chief architect will want to understand the whole building, but the business analyst or architect will certainly want a firm understanding of the top three floors. A business leader might only want to look at the business resources floor.

Let's take a walk down through the entire building, starting at the top.

Business and IT Services (A Logical View of the Business)

On the executive floor (see Figure 4.10), we can clearly see that this business offers a number of business services. These business services are supported by associated IT services. Currently, this level of description might be all we require. But you might notice that some of the Inventory links disappear down through the floor. If we follow these links, we can find out which part of the organization provides these services and what business data is used to support them. (As in many large organizations, there is a glass ceiling just below the executive floor…) This next floor down gives us a lot of information about the logical shape of the business (without specifying precisely what organizational elements or resources are involved in its execution).

Business Resources (A Physical View of the Business Combined with a Logical View of the IT)

On the floor below that, we are looking at the business from an operational perspective (see Figure 4.11). What resources are used to support the services we just looked at? On this floor, we can see that a number of different organizations, locations, systems, and databases support the business services and processes. The relationships between these resources are also clearly indicated on this floor. Many of these relationships are the existing business and IT constraints that we introduced in Chapter 1, "Eating Elephants Is Difficult." This is a pretty unique perspective that addresses many of the kinds of questions we often find difficult to answer. This is because this floor displays information that is usually found in separate Views maintained by different users. It is highly unusual to see it brought together in a single space. You'll also notice here that links go upward (to the business logical space) as well as downward.

Figure 4.10 On the executive floor, we can walk around the major functions that this business provides to its customers.

Figure 4.11 The business operations floor displays the resources that the business needs to meet its customers' needs.

The Machine Room (A Physical View of the IT)

Finally, in Figure 4.12, we make our way down into the machine room. All the systems and databases we identified on the floor above trace down to the physical machines (or clusters of machines) shown on this floor. Running between the machines are networks. From here, we can trace the impact of losing a machine or a location on the business that runs above us—a powerful perspective indeed.

Figure 4.12   In the bowels of the building, a virtual IT architect maintains the physical systems that underpin the business systems that support the business processes or provide the various channels for the customers or suppliers to interact with the business.

Of course, you'll notice that this isn't all of the Inventory. The whole point of generating such a visualization is that you can choose to display the elements that make sense to your audience. Chapter 9, "Inside the Elephant Eater," explains how to automatically extract high-level information from the detailed Inventory.

Indeed, the great beauty of this approach is that this visualization is just another Artifact generated from the Inventory. As the Inventory changes, the visualization will change when the Artifact is automatically regenerated. Such models take a trivial time to create because, unlike in PowerPoint, they draw themselves via self-organizing principles.

The capability to automatically harvest a series of Views from a site survey, combine those Views within an Inventory, and then use the Inventory to automatically generate an easy-to-understand 3D representation is a very powerful capability that makes the IT industry's current Greenfield approaches (manually abstracting the existing environment so it can be understood, manually refining this description over a long period of time, and then manually reabstracting it to PowerPoint to explain it to the business people) look very primitive indeed.

The most encouraging element about these kinds of visualizations is the reactions they get. "Cool!" is a common reaction (or "Supercool!" according to Grady Booch), but some regard them as things of aesthetic quality and beauty. We need some more of that in our industry. The visualizations can be created from any point, from the site survey onward. Thus, they are an excellent mechanism for communicating the understanding gained from "eating" the complexity of the surrounding environment. They're also an excellent way of presenting evolutionary options for any solution. We predict that within one generation, the IT industry will wonder how we built and collaborated on complex IT projects around the globe without them.

Endnotes

1 Cooperative Association for Internet Data Analysis. "Walrus Tool." www.caida.org/tools/visualization/walrus/gallery1/index.xml.

2 Munzner, Tamara. "H3 Viewer." http://graphics.stanford.edu/~munzner/h3/.

3 Linden Lab. Second Life. http://secondlife.com/.

4 Attributes are the individual elements of information that make up more complex structures, such as interfaces and data entities. Thus, value and date might be attributes of the Check entity or the getCheckDetails interface.

5 Use case models capture the behavior of an end user as it interacts with a system to complete a goal or task.

6 Classified business terms are clear and unambiguous definitions of key elements of the business terminology that is specific to the problem. They define a common vocabulary for the project.

7 Metadata is information about information, so business metadata is information about business data, such as its structure or its allowed contents—not the business data itself.

5

The Mythical Metaman

"There is no silver bullet."
—Fred P. Brooks, Jr.

Chapter Contents

- When You Eliminate the Impossible   91
- The Long Tail of Business Services   98
- Business Attractors for Attractive Businesses   104
- The Death of Brownfield   105
- Endnotes   105

The last four chapters described the Brownfield approach and showed how it can be used to reengineer complex environments. But this is just the initial application of Brownfield. By switching viewpoints from Greenfield to Brownfield and adopting the VITA architecture, further possibilities emerge. This chapter looks at the future of Brownfield and what it might ultimately mean for the IT industry.

By now, it should be easy to understand the applicability of Brownfield in terms of delivering large IT projects. So far, the focus has been on eating the IT elephant, per the title of the book. This perspective is deliberate. The best way to explain what Brownfield is about is to describe the problems it was designed to overcome. As a result, the book has so far primarily looked at how the Elephant Eater and the Brownfield approach can overcome environmental complexity and the communication problems of large projects.

The book has also examined how it is possible to create powerful new Inventories of information to store the environmental complexity, project requirements, and definition of a solution. In the more technical Part II, "The Elephant Eater," we explain the new semantic technologies underpinning these capabilities.

Semantic technologies are relatively new. They aim to provide new mechanisms for computers and humans to understand the context and meaning of the information they are dealing with. This makes communication less ambiguous, in much the same way that we clarified the word "check" in Chapter 3, "Big-Mouthed Superhero Required." This chapter looks at the further possibilities that the Brownfield technique offers when combined with these semantic technologies.

In *The Mythical Man Month,* Fred Brooks describes a "silver bullet" as a single measure that would raise the productivity of the IT industry tenfold. Many IT industry movements have claimed to be silver bullets over the years. None has realized such potential. As Grady Booch reiterates, "Software engineering is fundamentally hard." Brownfield does not change that. Brownfield is not a silver bullet.

It does, however, come closer to solving some of the intractable problems the IT industry has created for itself and businesses over the last 20 years. It is not a new way of writing programs, or a new architectural approach for functional decomposition, or a mechanism for ensuring code reuse. It is not a productivity enabler at heart, although significant project productivity gains of 40% or more have been measured. In contrast, it tries to answer a different question. The industry should not ask itself, "What can we do to be more efficient?" but fundamentally, "How do we turn today's inflexible systems into tomorrow's dynamic ones?" Brownfield is not a technology or an architecture—it's a fundamental change in looking at IT. It is how to cost-effectively realize the vision of business flexibility and interoperability that SOAs and Web 2.0 promise. If it is such a good enabler of known end goals, what other futures might it enable?

When You Eliminate the Impossible

Brownfield is such a compelling idea that, once it's in your head, you begin to wonder why it has never been used. Chapter 7, "Evolution of the Elephant Eater," shows that Brownfield is the aggregation of a number of existing IT techniques and some new ones—and explains why its time has come.

Many of these new techniques and technologies have been enabled for mainstream use by the popularity of XML and the investment currently being made in semantic technologies by Sir Tim Berners-Lee[1] and many others. These technologies likely will become mainstream.

In this chapter, therefore, we do a very dangerous thing: We look into the future of the IT industry and extrapolate what the combination of powerful semantic technologies and Brownfield might create. In doing so, remember that all predictions about the future of the IT industry are invariably wrong—possibly even this one. To maintain a level of credibility, therefore, we exclusively extrapolate from known capabilities.

Software Archaeologist Digs Up Babel Fish

Much of this book has looked at the capability to discover information about the problem being solved, reengineer that information to generate the solution, and test the solution. The initial envisioning for the Elephant Eater was that the Views being eaten would be at the level of formal design documentation. (It seemed sensible that the Views should be at a similar level as the UML or XML data sources that are increasingly used to specify both high-level and low-level designs.) This would mean that everyone involved in the design could continue to work as normal but would actually be creating Views suitable for feeding into the Elephant Eater.

By using these design-level sources of information, the business analysts, architects, and specialists could easily perform mappings between design-level concepts and could maintain and generate solutions to their problems. For example, the data entities that the business analysts recorded in the use cases could be formally linked (or mapped) onto the Logical Data Model created by the architect. Although the Views would be maintained separately in different tools, if they ever moved out of synchronization, the Elephant Eater would force them back into line.

This solution works well for much of what must be done, even in elephantine projects. Sometimes, however, projects get even harder. The environment might be so large or complex that even simple mapping between concepts becomes laborious and time consuming. Could Brownfield be used to accelerate this process of mapping concepts?

On one huge and complex project, we needed to precisely mimic part of the behavior of a very old legacy system to ensure that the system worked end to end. We knew where the information was, but the legacy system was undocumented and essentially unknown. The team that maintained and understood the system was too busy to talk to us because it was working flat out on a critical project to keep it going until we could replace it. It was a Catch-22 situation: We couldn't free up their time until we replaced their system, and we couldn't replace their system because they had no time to talk to us!

To make matters worse, the constraints that were hidden inside the same legacy system had caused all kinds of operational problems for the business when an earlier system had been sent live alongside the same legacy system. This was despite the fact that the new system had successfully completed its lengthy formal and expensive testing with flying colors. Unless we were going to suffer a similar fate, we needed a way to get at and understand the constraints and behavior of the legacy system so that our new system could work without disrupting the business.

Giving the task to the same team that had successfully parsed a host of other information for us, we expected a similar "one-off" answer to be proposed. What they came back with was far more exciting and powerful. Instead of simply analyzing the target system's code looking for certain keywords in certain contexts (simple static analysis), they suggested creating a representation of the whole program within the Inventory. When the whole program was in the Inventory, finding the information we were looking for would be much simpler.

—R.H. and K.J.

The idea of absorbing whole programs into the Inventory resulted in new uses for Brownfield tooling. The technique is called software archaeology. As described in more detail in Chapter 9, "Inside the Elephant Eater," software archaeology works by translating the legacy computer programs and configurations into a form that can be fed into the Inventory as a number of Views. As the legacy code is analyzed, it becomes possible to see its hidden structures, infer the original architecture, and even identify areas where that architecture has not been followed.

Ultimately, this technique could become the Babel fish[2] of computing architectures, enabling the shape of a legacy application to be determined by the archaeology tools and then regenerated using modern technologies. Although enhancements are still required to cope with the more dynamic aspects of some programs, these can be (and are being) addressed. The complexity of any program can be peeled away layer by layer until only the business logic remains. This isolated legacy business logic code can be analyzed and fed into a modern rules engine. The resulting business logic can then be advertised as a set of services, effectively turning a legacy application into an SOA.

This capability to automatically convert existing legacy spaghetti code efficiently into a flexible, modernized application is in its early days, but even at this stage, it looks hugely promising.

Radical Options for Business

As discussed in Chapter 3, Brownfield expands the scope of iterative development from being primarily focused on the user experience to encompassing the harder, less amorphous areas of integration and enterprise data. Brownfield effectively expands the IT industry's capability to use iterative techniques so that solutions can be defined incrementally within complex environments without creating a solution that is incompatible with its surroundings. Because this happens in a controlled way, business analysts have more power and techies have less. This is a good thing because business moves back into the driver's seat of IT projects.

Taking the approach further, perhaps ultimately this would result in businesses themselves becoming much more directly involved in specifying their own systems—and not through the artifice of being involved in designing and approving the user interface. The real business owners could look at real-time visualizations of their IT and business estate (like the ones in the last chapter), and use such visualizations to make decisions for both business and IT.

Ultimately, it might be possible for business leaders to walk around an editable visualization of their entire business (including their IT). Instead of just using the visualization to understand the business process and the IT environment that the business depends upon, they might be able to make changes to the representation. These changes would then create precise requirements for a business and IT reengineering project. In VITA terms, the visualization is generated as an Artifact, changed by the business leader, and fed back into the Elephant Eater as a View.

The implications of changing processes or IT systems could be immediately grasped from such multilayered displays. Feedback on the capability to enact the change could be calculated after analyzing the information in the Inventory. There's no reason why this analysis couldn't be done almost instantly. Suddenly, the capability to create a well-defined and implementable set of requirements would increase astronomically because all the constraints of the enterprise would be applied in real time. Coming up with good requirements for incrementally reengineering Brownfield sites is one of the hardest problems the IT industry has yet to solve. Perhaps this is the beginning of such a solution.

Taking this idea one step further, it might be possible to automatically ripple the impacts of high-level changes down through the Inventory—not only to assess the impact and disruption, but to actually regenerate the solution that runs the business. Furthermore, this might not require an architect or specialist, and it might not even directly change a single line of code. In such situations, the changes made in the business visualization could result in an automated change to the processes and software that run the business.

If so, the business would be in a very powerful position indeed. But how would it know which decisions to take?

Brownfield might expand to model not just the business and IT environment of the enterprise itself (as seen in Chapter 4, "The Trunk Road to the Brain"), but also its competitive environment. Within IBM's business analysis methods is an idea of modeling the business context and determining the external events that impact the business. If this black box boundary that defined the edges of a business was drawn a little bigger, could it provide an industry context instead?

Such all-encompassing black boxes are essentially ecosystems. Currently, they are hard to model and comprehend, but the extensibility of the Inventory suggests that such ecosystem modeling might be possible by drawing information from a huge variety of sources and using them as Views. Ultimately, these sources of information might be real-time feeds, making the projections dynamic forecasts.

The ultimate vision of Brownfield, therefore, is that it should be capable of iteratively changing and tuning business services within the context of the overall industry ecosystem. The business should be able to literally redraw an element of the business or introduce a new customer service, and immediately understand both how to underpin it with new or existing IT services and how it will impact the whole organism.

This expansion of agile capabilities should be seen as a continuation of the progress already made with Brownfield, as shown in Figure 5.1.

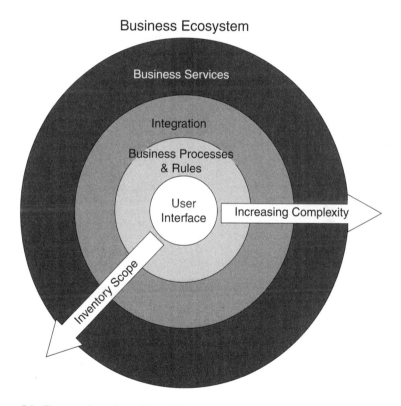

Figure 5.1 The expanding sphere of Brownfield.

Such reactive organisms have been called many things. Followers of IBM's major messages might recognize this kind of business "sense and respond" capability as On Demand. Sam Palmisano introduced this vision of On Demand when he took over as IBM CEO in 2000. Over the years, this vision became misinterpreted and was limited to a utility model for autonomic computing (buying computing power as needed it, as with electricity). The original vision, however, was one of business flexibility and integration.

As Palmisano predicted, such businesses would have a very powerful competitive advantage. Using the Brownfield approach, the business would potentially be able to rewire its Inventory using an intuitive visualization. By doing so, the business could regenerate systems and business processes. In such circumstances, the business leaders would be the true drivers of change, not the recipients of it.

Surely, then, this is the endpoint for Brownfield? Evolving the frozen elephant of yesteryear into the dancing elephants of tomorrow? Figure 5.2 graphically illustrates the point. In some ways, perhaps it is; this is certainly in line with the vision set out at the beginning of this book. Looking even farther down the Brownfield road, are there other sights to see?

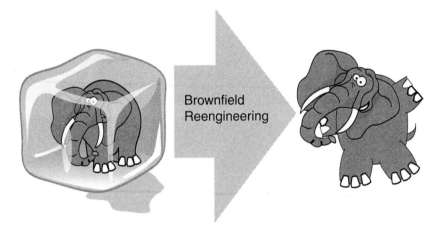

Figure 5.2   Over time, the frozen elephant could evolve into the dancing elephant.

At Your Service

Chapter 3 described some of what can be done with an Inventory and Transforms. The beauty and power of the Inventory lie in its simplicity. The capability to create multilevel, interrelated structures on top of it is a much closer corollary to the synaptic structures of the brain than conventional IT tooling. The kinds of structures that emerge within complex Inventories do not look that dissimilar to the structures we see in organic brains.

Because the language and structure of the Inventory have no artificial constraint (other than the ones imposed by choice), the VITA architecture is inherently extensible. Pretty much any formal documentation can be massaged into such a form held within its structure. Basically, triples are simple sentences and pretty much anything can be expressed in those terms, given enough thought (and enough sentences).

The likely outcome of this capability is twofold. First, hardware, operating systems, middleware, and applications will start being geared to provide information about themselves in formats ready for eating by the Elephant Eater. Hardware, operating systems, middleware, and applications will essentially be augmented to create standardized Views that describe their configuration. This will reduce the cost of doing an overarching full site survey, which currently would probably need to focus on the most difficult aspects of the problem to be cost-effective.

Second, that information will not need to be manually extracted from these sources, but will be available via open interfaces. The task of performing and updating the site survey of the existing environment will become automated and inexpensive rather than manual and prohibitive for simple areas.

Key aspects of this can already be seen in parts of the industry concerned with managing existing complexity—primarily the outsourcing and operations areas. IBM's Tivoli® Application Dependency Discovery Manager (TADDM) is a good example. TADDM works from the bottom up, automatically creating and maintaining application infrastructure maps. The TADDM application maps are comprehensive and include complete run-time dependencies, configuration values, and accurate change histories. For industries in which an application infrastructure audit is part of the legislative requirement for risk management (such as Basel II[3] in the finance industry), such tools are exceptionally useful.

TADDM currently stops at the application container (which runs the applications), but there's no particular reason why it needs to. The applications within the containers could be analyzed for further static relationships, even down to the code level.

Over time, therefore, we predict that the IT industry will move from the selected scything of information from Brownfield environments, to a combine harvesting approach in which the existing environment can be automatically eaten by the Elephant Eater to obtain a comprehensive description of its complexity.

The remodeling of both application and underlying middleware and hardware environments will become an iterative process of refinement.

The Long Tail of Business Services

The use of such standard harvesting tools will have a strong byproduct: The format of the Inventory itself and the classification of the information within it will begin to be standardized. Such formal classifications are called ontologies.

Ontologies are formal languages that can be used to unambiguously classify things, just like Venn diagrams (see Figure 5.3).

In Figure 5.3, everything is a Thing—except, of course, for the empty class Nothing. (This part of the classification is identical to the Web Ontology Language, OWL, which is one of the technical standards used for defining things in the Inventory.) Five further classifications (in bold) in the figure overlap in a complex pattern. These overlaps enable anything to be placed unambiguously on the diagram, defining its relationship with those five classifications. A quick analysis of Figure 5.3 enables us to confirm, for example, that the animal Tyrannosaurus Rex was large but did not have big ears and was a poor dancer.

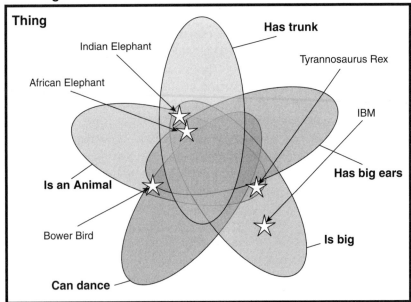

Figure 5.3 A five-set Venn diagram obsessed—like much of this book—with elephants.

As the coverage and depth of formal ontologies increase, computer systems will be able to change the way in which they communicate. Currently, computer systems communicate via interfaces that are defined by the format of the data they carry. In the future, as the use of Inventories and semantic technologies increases, the interfaces will be defined not in terms of the data formats in which they communicate, but in terms of the meaning. This means that the exact formats need not be known when the system is built. Ultimately, this enables connections between systems to be established that were not necessarily thought of when the communicating systems were built. If the systems can agree on what they want to talk about, they can create their own interfaces. Getting systems to talk together would no longer be a laborious process.

As the discovery tools used for Brownfield purposes increase in coverage and depth, they will help standardize many of the concepts and relationships within the Inventory. In other words, the vocabulary of the short sentences, the triples, will start to become common. What will the implication of such standardization be?

Enabling the Semantic Web

Sir Tim Berners-Lee's vision for the future of the Internet is the semantic Web, "a single Web of meaning, about everything and for everyone" whereas the Internet is billions of pages of information understood only by humans, the semantic Web would enable computers to understand the information on each page. You no longer would need to surf the Web to find the information you want; the semantically enabled search engines would be able to find it for you. In addition, writing programs to understand information on the Web and respond to it would become much easier.

The hard part, of course, is not working out how to publish and use semantic data. The hard part is getting people to agree with the same classifications and definitions, and getting them to link their data. This is difficult because the benefits of doing so are not immediately clear. As Berners-Lee himself points out, the benefit of the semantic Web is realized only when large quantities of data are available in these semantically strong ontology forms. Only then does everything click and the semantic Web provides a better way of interacting with customers or other organizations. Until that point, any investment in creating semantically strong Web resources is a burden to an organization. Currently, in commercial environments, this only amounts to a public show of faith in one particular future of the Web with little or no business benefit.

Using semantic technologies to create a site survey of existing Brownfield IT environments for potential change and regeneration means that the newly generated function created from the Inventory could automatically include additional semantic information. Adding this information would not be a burden; it would be a free byproduct of creating an Inventory that contains semantic information in the first place. Suddenly, the kind of additional information that the semantic Web needs to work would be available at little additional cost. IBM has measured significant productivity benefits from the use of its Elephant Eater, so we could make a strong business case for such reengineering.

Thus, publishing semantically based Web services that describe not only their content, but also the relationship of their content to other content becomes highly cost-effective. (The information is already there in the Inventory for the taking.) As a result, the kind of Web services companies offer would change forever.

Dynamic Services

In today's state-of-the-art implementations, IT services can be selected from a list of services in a directory. So if a company was looking for a trading partner that could offer a certain service, its inquiry to the directory service would be highly specific. The service would return only companies that had anticipated the inquiry. In the future, using semantic technologies would change such an interaction: The company would issue a request for a trading partner that offered a particular service, but instead of identifying matching services, the potential trading partners would see if they could assemble such a service—they would not need to have anticipated that particular request.

Geert-Willem Haasjes, a senior IT architect colleague from IBM in the Netherlands, has incorporated this model of flexible integration into a high-level architecture. Assuming that the requestor was trusted to access such a described service, the request for a trading partner would be returned via a service that had been constructed in real time to answer the specific request. Integration would become a dynamically established activity rather than a statically linked and formally tested service interface advertised via a directory of such static services.

Figure 5.4 shows the basic operation of such a system. In this figure, Enterprise A has followed the Brownfield approach. The organization's capabilities and constraints have been discovered and harvested in an Inventory. As a result, the services the business offers via the semantic Web exactly describe its capabilities (unlike those of its competitors).

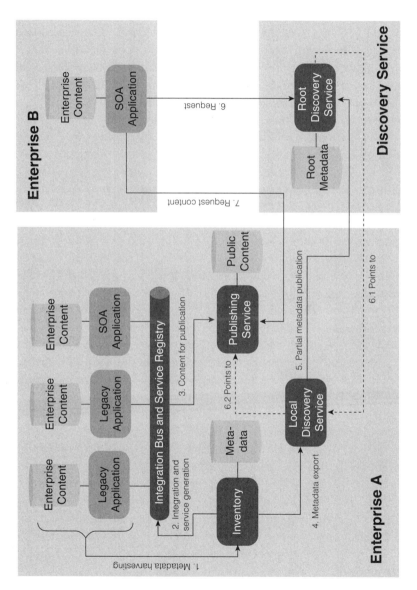

Figure 5.4 Enterprise B wants something unusual; Enterprise A can provide it.

Enterprise B is looking for a service but does not know how or where it can be serviced. Today, someone in Enterprise B would probably use Google to find a company specializing in that service and then use other forms of contact to establish whether the service required is exactly what the business wants—and how much it might cost. In this new world, a semantic-based request is sent. Instead of describing the precise form of the IT service that is required, the request describes the actual characteristics of the service itself. The request is sent to a search engine, which identifies that Enterprise A has published a service that is compatible with the request.

Enterprise B might have asked for something very unusual that Enterprise A has never received such a request for. But Enterprise A knows that it can meet the request because it knows about all its internal constraints. As a result, Enterprise A gets the business.

This kind of flexibility has a much bigger effect: Today's approach of delivering a set of specific products or services to a customer would completely break down. Once upon a time, your choice of what to buy was largely constrained by the store's capability to stock it. If you had a peculiar taste in music or literature, chances are, your local store wouldn't meet it. You might be able to order what you wanted, but if you wanted it urgently, you had to travel to a bigger store, or possibly travel even farther to find a specialist shop.

That pretty much all changed with the e-business revolution. These days, if it's made (and even if it's not), it likely can be ordered immediately via the Internet. Shops are no longer constrained by their physical footprint, so they can offer a greater variety to a much larger potential customer set via the Internet.

Chris Anderson pointed out this effect, known as the long tail, in 2004 and then popularized it in his book, *The Long Tail*.[4]

The long tail says that the amount of business available via low-volume sales might outweigh the amount of business available via high-volume sales (see Figure 5.5). Many Internet retailers make the bulk of their profit from the long tail, where they can attract higher levels of gross profit.

So why not have a long tail of business services for customers? Using the previous model, the customers could essentially customize the offering that they want, including the supporting business processes within the supplier organization.

If the retail industry model holds strong, these highly personalized and customized—and, therefore, desirable—products could offer significantly greater profit.

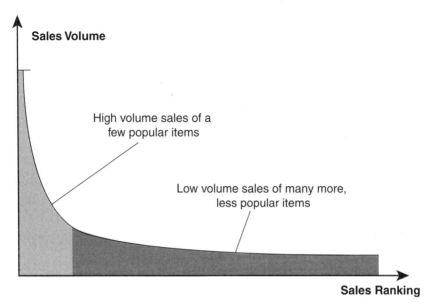

The area of the low volume items is greater than the area of the popular items.

Figure 5.5 Chris Anderson's long tail

Consider an example with the new BMW Mini: The number of options available almost ensures that each car is different from anyone else's. The car thus reflects the customer's individuality; the customer values this and sees it as a key differentiator in the market, enabling the company to charge a premium price for a small car.

Everything We Do Is Driven by You

Ultimately, therefore, the Brownfield vision is for businesses that are literally driven by their customers—not just at the macro level of determining what products and services their customers might like, but actually at the micro level of a customized offering that the customer has specifically asked for.

In such an environment, IT (as a separate department receiving requests from the business and acting on them) is dead. The translation layers and communication gaps between IT and the business have been removed. The IT is driven dynamically by the business and adapts automatically as required.

As a result, all businesses will need and use Inventories; they will be unable to compete without them. But when everyone has an Inventory, will this create a level playing field? Probably not. Whenever something unique is created, it is then copied and commoditized or standardized—and then something else comes along to improve on it. So in a world of Inventories, who would be king?

Business Attractors for Attractive Businesses

After the business, its processes, and its supporting IT are fed into the Inventory, the Inventory would contain thousands of Views. As predicted by Fred Brooks, Grady Booch, and a host of other IT thought leaders, the complexity of the Inventory would ensure that software engineering remained a complex pursuit.

Ultimately, the patterns, hidden knowledge, and capabilities in the Inventories will differentiate organizations. An organization's capability to mine, analyze, improve, and reengineer its own Inventory will become vital. In a fast-moving world, businesses that can identify and establish structures that can withstand the chaos around them will survive.

Such islands of strength will be akin to the strange attractors of chaos theory. Strange attractors define the long-term, complex, yet stable patterns that chaotic dynamic systems ultimately evolve into. Business environments are essentially dynamic chaotic systems: Even if you know an awful lot about the industry and its key players, it is still almost impossible to predict its future. As with the weather, predicting the future behavior of business environments is difficult. Even in such complex and unpredictable systems, however, there are islands of order. These strange attractors are ultimately the places where long-lived successful businesses will ultimately be drawn and thrive.

Unfortunately, only one kind of brain can cope with that amount of precise, complex, and interrelated information *and* model the surrounding chaos. It would be appropriate if this were an elephant's brain because they don't forget—but the truth is that computer programs will have to be written (or generated) to analyze and adapt the Inventories themselves.

In companies in which the business data, IT, and business processes are one—each coupled to the others in well-defined symbiotic ways—the entire organization begins to resemble an organism instead of a conventional business. This is the embodiment of an enterprise within a complex program that is aware of its businesses structure and its place within a wider business ecosystem. Such a being would be capable of dealing with chaos and an uncertain future. Computer programs called Inventory optimizers could be used to constantly adapt the business to its ecosystem.

Just as chaos theory has taught us that hidden within apparent disorder, such as weather patterns, are complex patterns of stability, these Inventory optimizers would look for stable business attractors within their chaotic and dynamically changing ecosystem. Businesses that conformed to such attractors would be uniquely capable of surfing on the very edge of constantly changing waves of change without losing their fundamental structure or order.

Gregory Stock invented a similar concept in his book *Metaman: The Merging of Humans and Machines into a Global Superorganism.*[5] The metaman is a market-driven hugely robust superorganism that includes both human and technological components that ultimately dominates mankind's future. It's a fundamentally optimistic book, so perhaps it's not a bad note on which to end this part of the book. Brownfield takes over the world!

The Death of Brownfield

Of course, by the time the world gets to the metaman, such an ecosystem would have long ago reengineered every other system in the enterprise and optimized every process. As the world around it changes, the metaman will analyze the new landscape in real time and adapt itself accordingly. In such environments, the IT would be reengineered at its will—every day there could be a new environment.

Perhaps that's the ultimate fate of Brownfield. If Brownfield succeeds, there will be no IT Brownfields anymore—no environmental constraints, no 500-person-year projects effecting change at a snail's pace. We can hope... and, in the meantime, we shall keep trying.

Endnotes

[1] Sir Tim Berners-Lee founded the Web, not the Internet, which was founded much earlier.

[2] The Babel fish is an invention of the late and much lamented Douglas Adams. It was a creature that, if you stuck it in your ear, it would automatically translate everything you heard in any language.

[3] Basel II offers recommendations for banking law and regulation, to ensure that banks remain financially stable in the face of the risks they take.

[4] Anderson, Chris. *The Long Tail.* NY/NY/USA: Hyperion, 2006.

[5] Stock, Gregory. *Metaman: The Merging of Humans and Machines into a Global Superorganism.* NY/NY/USA: Simon & Schuster, 1993.

PART **II**

The Elephant Eater

Chapter 6 ▪ Abstraction Works Only in a Perfect World

Chapter 7 ▪ Evolution of the Elephant Eater

Chapter 8 ▪ Brownfield Development

Chapter 9 ▪ Inside the Elephant Eater

Chapter 10 ▪ Elephant Eater at Work

6

Abstraction Works Only in a Perfect World

"There is no abstract art. You must always start with something. Afterward you can remove all traces of reality."
—*Pablo Picasso*

Chapter Contents

- Considerations for an Elephant Eater   110
- Systems Integration and Engineering Techniques   112
- Abstraction Is the Heart of Architecture   118
- Do We Need a Grand Unified Tool?   128
- The Connoisseur's Guide to Eating Elephants   129
- Endnotes   131

In the first part of the book, we saw how IT systems have grown increasingly larger and more complex over time. This growing complexity is challenging the capability of businesses to innovate as more of the IT budget is channeled into regulatory compliance, replatforming, and maintenance of the status quo. As this book has shown, changing these systems is not primarily a technical difficulty, but one of coordinating and disambiguating human communication. In overcoming such difficulties, we have introduced the concept of an Elephant Eater and the Brownfield development approach.

This second part of the book explains the technical and practical aspects of Brownfield for someone who might want to implement such an approach. This chapter examines the necessary technical context, requirements, and characteristics of the Elephant Eater. The chapter then goes on to analyze existing IT elephant-eating approaches and highlights the problems these approaches present with their extensive use of decomposition and abstraction.

Considerations for an Elephant Eater

The following sections outline considerations for the Elephant Eater. The problems with large scale developments are many, and the first half of the book illustrated some of the problems that such developments pose. The high failure rate for such projects is the reason why the creation of an Elephant Eater was necessary. Like any problem, the starting point for a solution is the understanding of the requirements, so if an Elephant Eater is going to be created, it needs to cater to the considerations in this section.

Lack of Transparency

On very large-scale developments, the problem being solved usually is unclear. At a high level, the design and development task might seem to be understood—for example, "build a family home," "design a hospital," or "implement a customer relationship management system." However, such terms are insufficient to describe what is actually required.

For any complex problem, some degree of analysis and investigation is essential to properly frame the detailed requirements of the solution and understand its context. In conventional building architectures, the site survey is a fundamental part of the requirements-gathering process.

A thorough analysis of a complex site takes a great deal of time and effort. Even using traditional Greenfield methods, the analysis effort is often as large as the build effort. Despite this effort, however, IT architects and business analysts rarely do as thorough a job of surveying a site as building architects do. As discussed in previous chapters, a thorough analysis that encompasses functional and nonfunctional requirements and multiple constraints requires vast documentation. As such, the real requirements in any situation are always less than transparent.

Unfortunately, in IT, relatively little time is spent on the equivalent of a site survey.

Multiple Conflicting Goals

Another problem is conflicting requirements. In any complex situation, a single optimal solution is rarely a given for such a problem. The problem itself might even be poorly described.

In the example of the house building discussion in Chapter 1, "Eating Elephants Is Difficult," the mother-in-law and the landowner could have very different perspectives on what is desirable. Will their combined requirements be entirely coherent and compatible? Whose job will it be to resolve these conflicts?

We have seen the same problem on multiple $100 million programs. Any big program owned by more than one powerful stakeholder is likely to fail because of confusing and conflicted directions. As we saw in Chapter 1, life is much easier when one powerful person is consistently in charge. Of course, assigning a single stakeholder is not easy, but failing to identify this stakeholder at the start of the project only ignores the problem.

Spotting requirements that are clearly expressed but in conflict is reasonably easy, and it is usually possible to resolve these through careful negotiation. No one would seriously demand two mutually incompatible set of requirements, right?

Let's return to the analogy of home building as an example. When designing a house, increasing the size of the windows will increase the feeling of light and space within the building and improve the view. But bigger windows will contribute to energy loss. Improved insulation in the walls or ceilings might compensate for this, but this could result in increased building costs or a reduced living area. Alternatively, the architect could request special triple glazing. That would make the windows more thermally efficient but could make the glass less translucent. As more concerns arise, the interplays between them become more complex. As a result, the final solution becomes a trade-off between different aspects or characteristics of the solution. Possibly, the requirements are actually mutually incompatible—but this can be known only in the context of a solution.

These conflicting requirements also come up repeatedly when designing large computer systems. We hear comments similar to these: "We need the system to be hugely scaleable to cope with any unexpected demand. It must be available 24 hours a day, 7 days a week—even during upgrades or maintenance—but must be cheaper to build, run, and maintain than the last system." Obviously, such requirements are always in conflict.

Dynamic Aspects

The difficulty in coping with these requirements is compounded by the fact that they don't stand still. As you begin to interfere and interact with the problem, you change it. For example, talking to a user about what the system currently does could change that user's perception about what it needs to do. Interacting with the system during acceptance testing might overturn those initial perceptions again. Introducing the supposed solution into the environment could cause additional difficulties.

In IT systems, these side effects often result from a lack of understanding that installing a new IT system changes its surroundings. Subsequent changes also might need to be made to existing business procedures and best practices that are not directly part of the solution. These changes might alter people's jobs, their interaction with customers, or the skills they require.

In addition to these impacts, the time involved in such projects usually means that the business environment in which the solution is to be placed has evolved. Some of the original requirements might need to change or might no longer be applicable

Therefore, one of the key requirements for any Elephant Eater is tight and dynamic linkage between the business and IT.

Systems Integration and Engineering Techniques

But the problem we're talking about isn't new, is it? People have been trying to deliver complex systems for more than 40 years. There must already be some pretty reasonable Elephant Eaters out there.

Now that we have a good understanding of the problem, it's a good idea to take a closer look at some of the solutions that are already out there and see why, given the meager 30 percent success rate noted in the Preface, we need a new Elephant Eater.

Generally, these big problems need to be approached via formal techniques. These techniques work from two different directions. They either work their way down from the top, gaining increasing levels of detail, or they start from the bottom, examining needs in detail and working their way upward, building toward a complete solution.

Walk the Easy Path or...

If you're infinitely lucky, the bottom-up approach might work. Considering a very simple example, you could select a package that seems close to what you need. You could then walk through the business processes you want to execute. As you go, you can write down all the changes you need to make to the package, and, *presto!* After you've made the changes, you've got a solution! You've designed the whole system from the ground up because the package dictates your choices for how you do pretty much everything else.

If you don't allow the package to dictate your choices, chances are, you will find yourself in a very sticky mess: Each major change you make will require extra development, testing, and long-term maintenance costs. If you've chosen the bottom-up approach, you must stick to it religiously and accept the changes it will impose on the process and the business.

Ultimately, a package with a good fit, whether imposed or a lucky choice, is the very best in bottom-up solutions. Start halfway up the hill—the package already approximates what you want. Then modify the solution iteratively with the end user and find a happy endpoint near the top of the hill.

However, chances are, for a really complex project, using the bottom-up approach with a single package will not work. You must break down the problem into smaller pieces and then integrate them to create a single solution. You can divide up the problem in two fundamental ways.

...Break the Boulders and Make Them Smooth

You can decompose the problem into smaller, more easily managed Views through two methods: splitting and abstraction. Splitting simply divides complex big chunks into smaller, more manageable pieces. Abstraction removes detail from each larger chunk to form more manageable and understandable pieces. These two techniques, splitting and abstraction, allow almost any gargantuan problem to be subdivided into smaller, better contained problems. Think of it as slicing the problem into little squares.

Abstraction gives you horizontal cuts, while View splitting gives you vertical ones. Everything becomes a manageable "chunk." This is the basis for most systems integration and engineering methods. Many of these methods are proprietary, but some, such as The Open Group Architecture Framework (TOGAF) from the Open Foundation, are freely available. Each approach tries to create a continuum of knowledge, from high-level representations to more detailed. These paths vary but can be characterized as moving in some way from logical to physical, general to specific, or taxonomy to specification.

When good methods or tools are used, there is traceability from the high level to the low level. This helps a reader understand why something has been designed the way it has.

Such movement is unsurprisingly characterized as a progression, starting from the high-level principles and overall vision of what needs to be achieved, and moving down through the perspectives of business, process, roles, and models of information. Figure 6.1 highlights the basic stages of the TOGAF method.

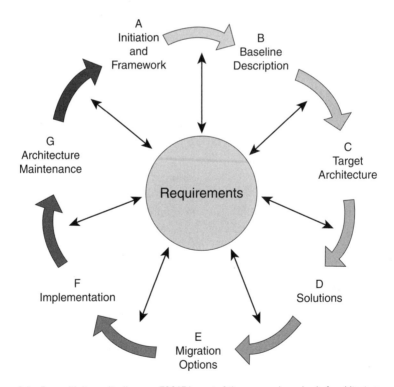

Figure 6.1 Even with its cyclic diagram, TOGAF is part of the progressive school of architecture.

Some approaches go even further. They segment each level of abstraction into a number of separate perspectives. Of these "frameworks," the enterprise architecture framework produced by John Zachman of IBM in the 1980s is probably the most famous. Called the Zachman Framework, it considers the additional dimension of Data, Function, Network, People, Time, and Motivation. Figure 6.2 illustrates how the Zachman Framework segments the architecture into these perspectives.

	What? Data	How? Function	Where? Network	Who? People	When? Time	Why? Motivation	
Planner							Scope
Owner							Enterprise Models
Designer							System Models
Builder							Technology Models
Sub- contractor							Detailed Represent- ations
Enterprise							Actual Systems

Figure 6.2   The Zachman Framework of Enterprise Architecture segments the architecture into a variety of perspectives.

These approaches enable you to decompose the full width and breadth of the problem (including the existing constraints) into separate Views so that a suitably skilled guru can independently govern and maintain them.

At the very top of this top-down approach is a simple sheet of paper that purports to show or describe the scope of the whole problem for that particular perspective. A single sheet of paper might even purport to summarize the 10,000-foot view for *all* the perspectives.

Below that top sheet are many more sheets that describe each element on the sheet above. This technique is so well recognized that it's applied to almost everything in complex problems, whether we're talking about the shape of the system, the business processes that it executes, or the description of the plan that will build it.

In this hierarchy of paper, the top tier is labeled Level 0; the next tier down, Level 1; and so on. At each layer, the number of sheets of paper increases, but each of these sheets is a manageable View. The problem has been successfully decomposed. In the example in Figure 6.3, our single-page business context that describes the boundaries of the problem we're solving is gradually decomposed into 60,000 pages of code, deployment information, and operational instructions that describe the whole solution. At each step of the way, the intermediate representations all correspond to a View.

After the problem has been decomposed into single sheets, or Views, rules must be written and applied to specify how they work together.

Surely that solves our problem. The elephant has been eaten. Complexity is reduced, so each area becomes manageable. Each person is dealing with only a bit of the problem.

This is, of course, precisely what the world's largest systems integrators do. They define their Views in terms of work products or deliverables. They come from different perspectives and at different levels of abstraction. The systems integrators have design and development methods that describe who should do what to which View (or work product) and in what order.

So if the problem is essentially solved, why does it go wrong so often?

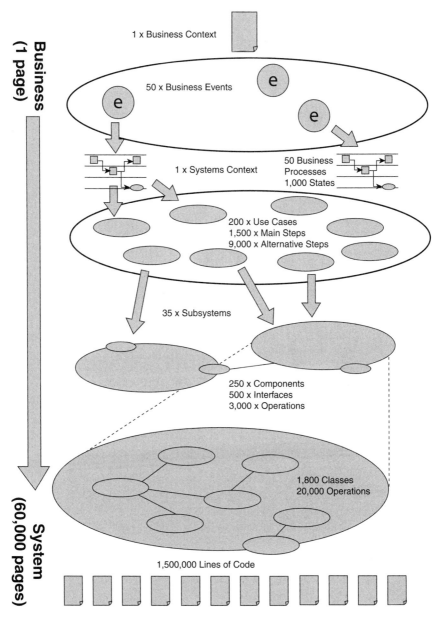

Figure 6.3 Decomposition of a complex problem space

Abstraction Is the Heart of Architecture

In all these cases, we move from the general to the specific, with the next layer of detail expanding upon the previous level of abstraction. This movement from general to specific gives architecture its power to simplify, communicate, and make ghastly complexity more aesthetically pleasing.

Abstraction is the heart of architecture. This powerful and persuasive concept has been at the center of most of the advances in complex systems architecting for the last 15 years. It underpins the history of software engineering—objects, components, and even IT services have their roots in abstraction. Because abstraction is one of our most powerful tools, we should consider its capabilities and limitations.

As systems have become more complex, additional layers of abstraction have been inserted into the software to keep everything understandable and maintainable. Year by year, programmers have gotten further away from the bits, registers, and native machine code, through the introduction of languages, layered software architectures, object-oriented languages, visual programming, modeling, packages, and even models of models (metamodeling).

Today, programs can be routinely written, tested, and deployed without manually writing a single line of code or even understanding the basics of how a computer works. A cornucopia of techniques and technologies can insulate today's programmers from the specifics and complexities of their surrounding environments. Writing a program is so simple that we can even get a computer to do it. We get used to the idea of being insulated from the complexity of the real world.

Mirror, Mirror on the Wall, Which Is the Fairest Software of All?

Software engineering approaches the complexity and unpredictability of the real world by abstracting the detail to something more convenient and incrementally improving the abstraction over time.

Working out the levels of abstraction that solve the problem (and will continue to solve the problem) is the key concern of the software architect. IBM's chief scientist Grady Booch and other leaders of the software industry are convinced that the best software should be capable of dealing with great complexity but also should be inherently simple and aesthetically pleasing.[1]

Thus, over time, we should expect that increasing levels of abstraction will enable our software to deal with more aspects of the real world. This is most obviously noticeable in games and virtual worlds, where the sophistication of the representation of the virtual reality has increased as individual elements of the problem are abstracted. Figure 6.4 shows how games architectures have matured over the last 20 years.

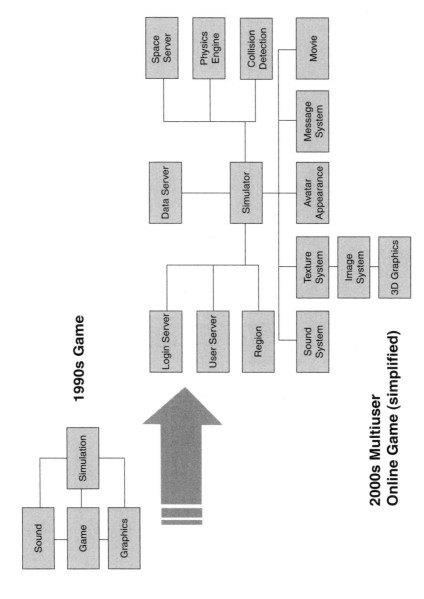

Figure 6.4 Games architectures have matured immensely over the last 20 years.

The current sophisticated, shared online games of the early twenty-first century exhibit greater descriptive power compared to the basic 2D games of the 1970s. Hiding the complexity of the physics engine from the graphical rendering system, and hiding both of these from the user server and the system that stores the in-world objects, enables increasing levels of sophisticated behavior.

Abstraction has its drawbacks, however. Each level of abstraction deliberately hides a certain amount of complexity. That's fine if you start with a complete description of the problem and work your way upward, but you must remember that this isn't the way today's systems integration and architecting methods work.

These methods start from the general and the abstract, and gradually refine the level of detail from there. Eventually, they drill down to reality. This sounds good. Superficially, it sounds almost like a scientific technique. For example, physicists conduct experiments in the real world, which has a lot of complexity, imperfection, and "noise" complicating their experiments. However, those experiments are designed to define or confirm useful and accurate abstractions of reality in the form of mathematical theories that will enable them to make successful predictions. Of course, the key difference between software engineering and physics is that the physicists are iteratively creating abstractions for something that already exists and refining the abstraction as more facts emerge. The architects, on the other hand, are abstracting first and then creating the detail to slot in behind the abstraction. Figure 6.5 should make the comparison clearer.

The IT approach should strike you as fundamentally wrong. If you need some convincing, instead of focusing on the rather abstract worlds of physics or IT, let's first take a look at something more down to earth: plumbing.

Plumbing the Depths

The IT and plumbing industries have much in common. Participants in both spend a great deal of time sucking their teeth, saying, "Well, I wouldn't have done it like that," or, "That'll cost a few dollars to put right." As in many other professions, they make sure that they shroud themselves in indecipherable private languages, acronyms, and anecdotes.

Figure 6.5   Who's right? Physicists or IT architects?

Imagine for a moment a heating engineer who has been asked to install a radiator in a new extension. He has looked at the plans and knows how he's going to get access to the pipes. From the specifications he's read, he knows what fixtures he needs. After doing some pretty easy calculations based on room size, window area, and wall type, he even got hold of the right size radiator to fit on the wall that will deliver the right amount of heat for the room. It's an hour's work, at most.

The job is done and he leaves a happy man. A few days later, the homeowner is complaining that the room is still cold. Only when the plumber arrives back on-site and investigates the boiler does he find out that the output of the boiler is now insufficient for the needs of the house. He recommends that the homeowner order a new 33-kilowatt boiler and arranges to come back in a week.

A week later, he's back to begin fitting the new boiler. Right at the start of the task, it becomes obvious that the old boiler was oil-fired and the new one is gas. This is slightly inconvenient because the property is not connected to the gas main, even though it runs past the property.

Another few weeks pass while the homeowner arranges for the house to be connected to the gas supply. On the plumber's third visit, everything is going swimmingly. Then he notices that there are no free breaker slots on the electricity circuit board to attach the new boiler. A week later, he replaces the circuit board. The boiler is installed, but another problem arises: Although the heat output of the boiler is sufficient, a more powerful pump is required to distribute the heat throughout the house.

And that's when the problems really start.

Don't Abstract Until You See the Whole Elephant

Judging from the architect's top-level view, the solution seemed pretty obvious. Only when the job was almost done was it obvious that it hadn't worked. Those other aspects of the problem—the supply, the pump, and the circuit board—were invisible from the Level 0 perspective the plumber received, so he ignored them in doing his analysis.

After all, nothing was fundamentally wrong with the plumber's solution; he just didn't have a good specification of the problem. The process of abstracting the problem to the single architectural drawing of the new room meant that he had no visibility of the real problem, which was somewhat bigger and more complex. He simply couldn't see the hidden requirements—the environmental constraints—from his top-level, incorrectly abstracted view of the problem.

Unfortunately, abstractions, per se, always lack details of the underlying complexity. The radiator was a good theoretical solution to the problem, but it was being treated as a simple abstract component that, when connected to the central heating system, would issue the right amount of heat. Behind that simple abstraction lays the real hidden complexity of the boiler, gas main, and circuit board that leaked through and derailed this abstracted solution.[2] Will such complexity always leak up through the pipe and derail simple abstract solutions?

Well, imagine for a moment that the abstraction was absolute and that it was impossible to trace backward from the radiator to the source of the heat. Consider, for example, that the heat to each radiator was supplied from one of a huge number of central utilities via shared pipes. If the complexity of that arrangement was completely hidden, you would not know who to complain to if the radiator didn't work. Of course, on the positive side, the utility company supplying your heat wouldn't be able to bill you for adding a new radiator!

Is this such an absurd example? Consider today's IT infrastructures, with layers of software, each supposedly easier to maintain by hiding the complexities below. Who do you call when there is a problem? Is it in the application? The middleware? Maybe it is a problem with the database?

If you become completely insulated from the underlying complexity—or if you simply don't understand it, then it becomes very difficult to know what is happening when something goes wrong. Such an approach also encourages naïve rather than robust implementations. Abstractions that fully hide complexity ultimately cause problems because it is impossible to know what is going wrong.

Poorly formed abstractions can also create a lack of flexibility in any complex software architecture. If the wrong elements are chosen to be exposed to the layers above, people will have to find ways around the architecture, compromising its integrity. Establishing the right abstractions is more of an art than a science, but starting from a point of generalization is not a good place to start—it is possibly the worst.

Successful Abstraction Does Not Come from a Lack of Knowledge

In summary, abstraction is probably the single most powerful tool for the architect. It works well when used with care and when there is a deep understanding of the problem.

However, today's methods work from the general to the specific, so they essentially encourage and impose a lack of knowledge. Not surprisingly, therefore, the initial abstractions and decompositions that are made at the start of a big systems integration or development project often turn out to be wrong. Today's methods tend to ignore complexity while purporting to hide it.

The Ripple Effect

Poor abstractions lead to underestimations and misunderstandings galore. Everything looks so simple from 10,000 feet. On large projects, a saying goes that "All expensive mistakes are made on the first day." From our experience, it's an observation that is very, very true.

Working with a lack of information makes abstraction easy but inaccurate.

All projects are most optimistic right at the start. These early stages lack detailed information; as a result, assumptions are made and the big abstractions are decided.

Assumptions are not dangerous in themselves—as long as they are tracked. Unfortunately, all too often they are made but not tracked, and their impact is not understood. In some ways, they are treated as "risks that will never happen." Assumptions must always be tracked and reviewed, and their potential impact, if they're untrue, must be understood. Chances are, some of them will turn out to be false assumptions—and, chances are, those will be the ones with expensive consequences.

We need to move away from this optimistic, pretty-diagram school of architecture, in which making the right decisions is an art form of second guessing based on years of accumulated instinct and heuristics.[3] We need a more scientific approach with fewer assumptions and oversimplifications. A colleague, Bob Lojek, memorably said, "Once you understand the full problem, there is no problem."

Fundamentally, we need to put more effort into understanding the problem than prematurely defining the solution. As senior architects for IBM, we are often asked to intervene in client projects when things have gone awry. For example:

An Agile development method was being used to deliver a leading-edge, web-based, customer self-service solution for a world-leading credit card processor. The team had all the relevant skills, and the lead architect was a software engineering guru who knew the modern technology platform they were using and had delivered many projects in the past.

Given the new nature of the technology, the team had conformed strictly to the best-practice patterns for development and had created a technical prototype to ensure that the technology did what they wanted it to do. The design they had created was hugely elegant and was exactly in line with the customer requirement.

A problem arose, though. The project had run like a dream for 6 months, but it stalled in the final 3 months of the development. The reporting system for the project recorded correctly that 80 percent of the code had been written and was working, but the progress meter had stopped there and was not moving forward. IBM was asked to take a look and see what the problem was.

As usual, the answer was relatively straightforward. The levels of abstraction, or layering, of the system had been done according to theoretical best practice, but it was overly sophisticated for the job that needed to be done. The architecture failed the Occam's Razor test: The lead architect had induced unnecessary complexity, and his key architectural decisions around abstraction (and, to some extent, decomposition) of the problem had been made in isolation of the actual customer problem.

Second, and more important, the architect had ignored the inherent complexity of the solution. Although the user requirements were relatively straightforward and the Level 0 architecture perspectives were easy to understand, he had largely ignored the constraints imposed by the other systems that surrounded the self-service solution.

Yes, the design successfully performed a beautiful and elegant abstraction of the core concepts it needed to deal with—it's just that it didn't look anything like the systems to which it needed to be linked. As a result, the core activity for the previous 3 months had been a frantic attempt to map the new solution onto the limitations of the transactions and data models of the old. The mind-bending complexity of trying to pull together two mutually incompatible views of these new and old systems had paralyzed the delivery team. They didn't want to think the unthinkable. They had defined an elegant and best-practice solution to the wrong problem. In doing so, they had ignored hundreds of constraints that needed to be imposed on the new system.

When the project restarted with a core understanding of these constraints, it became straightforward to define the right levels of abstraction and separation of concerns. This provided an elegant and simple solution with flexibility in all the right places—without complicating the solution's relationship with its neighbors.

—R.H.

As a final horror story, consider a major customer case system for an important government agency:

We were asked to intervene after the project (in the hands of another systems integrator) had made little progress after 2 years of investment.

At this point, the customer had chosen a package to provide its overarching customer care solution. After significant analysis, this package had been accepted as a superb fit to the business and user requirements. Pretty much everything that was needed to replace the hugely complex legacy systems would come out of a box.

However, it was thought that replacing a complete legacy system would be too risky. As a result, the decision was made to use half of the package for the end-user element of the strategic solution; the legacy systems the package was meant to replace would serve as its temporary back end (providing some of the complex logic and many of the interfaces that were necessary for an end-to-end solution).

The decision was to eat half the elephant. On paper, from 10,000 feet, it looked straightforward. The high-level analysis had not pointed out any glitches, and the layering of the architecture and the separation of concerns appeared clean and simple.

As the project progressed, however, it became apparent that the legacy system imposed a very different set of constraints on the package. Although they were highly similar from an end user and data perspective, the internal models of the new and old systems turned out to be hugely different—and these differences numbered in the thousands instead of the hundreds.

Ultimately, the three-way conflict between the user requirements (which were based on the promise of a full new system), the new package, and the legacy system meant that something had to give. The requirements were deemed to be strategic and the legacy system was immovable, so the package had to change. This decision broke the first rule of bottom-up implementations mentioned earlier.

Although the system was delivered on time and budget, and although it works to this day for thousands of users and millions of customers, the implementation was hugely complicated by the backflow of constraints from the legacy systems. As a result, it then proved uneconomic to move the system to subsequent major versions of the package. The desired strategic solution became a dead end.

—K.J. and R.H. _____

In each of these cases, a better and more detailed understanding of the overall problem was needed than standard top-down approaches could provide. Such an understanding would have prevented the problems these projects encountered.

Each of these three problems stems from a basic and incorrect assumption by stakeholders that they could build a Greenfield implementation. At the credit card processor, this assumption held firm until they tried to integrate it with the existing infrastructure. The government department failed to realize that its original requirements were based on a survey of a completely different site (the one in which the legacy system was cleared away), resulting in large-scale customization of the original package that was supposedly a perfect fit.

Fundamentally, today's large-scale IT projects need to work around the constraints of their existing environment. Today's IT architects should regard themselves as Brownfield redevelopers first, and exciting and visionary architects second.

Companies that try to upgrade their hardware or software to the latest levels experience the same ripple effect of contamination from the existing environment. Despite the abstraction and layering of modern software and the imposed rigor of enterprise architectures, making changes to the low levels of systems still has a major impact on today's enterprises.

As we mentioned before, no abstraction is perfect and, to some extent, it will leak around the edges. This means there is no such thing as a nondisruptive change to any nontrivial environment. As a supposedly independent layer in the environment changes—perhaps a database, middleware, or operating system version—a ripple of change permeates around the environment.

As only certain combinations of products are supported, the change can cascade like a chain of dominoes. Ultimately, these ripples can hit applications, resulting in retesting, application changes, or even reintegration.

Thus, to provide good and true architectures, we need to accept that we need a better understanding of the problem to engineer the right abstractions. Additionally, we need all the aspects of the problem definition (business, application, and infrastructure) to be interlinked so that we can understand when and where the ripple effect of discovered constraints or changes will impact the solution we are defining.

Do We Need a Grand Unified Tool?

The problem definition is too big for one tool or person to maintain, so there appears to be a dilemma. The full complexity of the problem needs to be embraced, and an understanding is required of everything that's around, including the existing IT and business environments. But all that information needs to be pulled together so that the Views aren't discrete or disconnected.

Many people have argued for tool unification as a means to achieve this, to maintain all these connected Views in a single tool and, thus, enable a single documented version of the truth to be established and maintained. But that is missing a vital point about Views.

As explained in Chapter 2, "The Confusion of Tongues," Views need to be maintained by people in their own way, in their own language. Imposing a single tool will never work. Simply too many preferred perspectives, roles, and prejudices exist within our industry to believe that everyone is going to sit down one day and record and maintain their Views in one specific tool.[4] If such combinations of Views into single multipurpose tools were possible, desirable, and usable, then it is arguable that Microsoft® Office user interfaces Word®, PowerPoint®, and Excel® would have merged long ago.

Moreover, these integrated approaches that have been at the heart of traditional tooling are usually pretty poor at dealing with ambiguity or differences of opinion. On large projects with many people working on the same information, it is not unusual to have formal repositories that enable people to check out information, make changes to it, and then check it back in. Such systems prevent two people from updating the same information at the same time, which would result in confusion and conflicts. The upshot of this approach, however, is that the information that is checked into the repository is the information that everyone else is then forced to use. The implications of your changes are not always apparent to you—or perhaps immediately to your colleagues, either. Maintaining a single source of truth when hundreds of people are changing individual overlapping elements is less than straight-forward. A change made by one individual can have serious consequences for many other areas of the project, and no mechanism exists for highlighting or resolving ambiguity—whoever checks the information into the repository last wins!

In summary, grand unified tools are to software engineering what grand unified theories are to modern physics—tricky to understand, multidimensional, and elusive, often involving bits of string. No one has created a single tool to maintain the full complexity of a complex IT project. Likewise, no one will do so unless the tool enables people to maintain Views in their own way, in their own language, and to identify and deal with ambiguity cooperatively.

The Connoisseur's Guide to Eating Elephants

This chapter set out to define the kinds of things the Elephant Eater must do, the kinds of problems it needs to deal with, and the kinds of environments with which it must cope. We've covered a lot of ground, so it's worth recapping the key requirements that we have established—a connoisseur's guide to eating elephants.

The Elephant Eater machine must recognize that the environment imposes many more constraints beyond functional and nonfunctional requirements. We rarely work on Greenfield sites anymore; the elephant-eating machine must be at home on the most complex Brownfield sites—the kind of Brownfield sites that have had a lot of IT complexity built up layer on layer over many years.

The Elephant Eater must also address the lack of transparency that is inherent within our most complex projects. This will enable us to x-ray our elephant to see the heart of the problem. To achieve this transparent understanding, the Elephant Eater must acknowledge the fundamental human limitation of the View and enable us to break down the problem into smaller chunks.

However, we suspect that a one-size-fits-all approach to maintaining Views is doomed to failure. A high-level business process View will always look very different than a detailed data definition. Therefore, an elephant-eating machine that relies on a single tool for all users is pretty impractical.

In addition, we now know that, despite the best efforts of architects to keep them insulated and isolated via abstractions and enterprise architectures, many of these Views are interlinked. Therefore, the only way to understand the problem properly is to make the interconnections between Views explicit and try to make them unambiguous. We should also note, however, that establishing a consolidated picture of all these Views needs to be a process of cooperation and communication—one View cannot overwrite another one, and ambiguity must be dealt with within its processing. We also know that the View should cover the entire solution (business, application, and infrastructure).

By using the formal View and VITA approach introduced in Part I, "Introducing Brownfield," it should be possible to see how the Elephant Eater proposed can address these requirements. The following facets are an intrinsic part of Brownfield development.

Our Brownfield abstractions—and, therefore, architectures—will be a good fit for the problem: Those decisions will be made based on detailed information fed in via a site survey instead of vague generalization. This adopts an engineer's approach to the solution instead of the artisan's heuristics and intuition.

We will be able to preempt the ripple effect, often understanding which requirements are in conflict or at least knowing the horrors hiding behind the constraints. Therefore, the requirements can be cost-effectively refined instead of the abstractions of the solution or its code. Resolving these problems early will have significant economic benefit.

The solution will become easier to create due to a deeper understanding of the problem. A precise and unambiguous specification will enable the use of delivery accelerators such as these:

- Global delivery and centers of excellence
- Code generation via Model Driven Development and Pattern Driven Engineering because the precise specification can be used to parameterize the generation processes
- Iterative delivery as possible strategies for appropriate business and IT segmentation of the problem become clearer

Therefore, the Brownfield approach conceptually solves many of the problems presented in this chapter and previous chapters, avoiding the early, unreliable, and imprecise abstractions and decompositions of existing approaches. In the remaining chapters, we examine how Brownfield evolved and how it can be deployed on large-scale IT projects.

Endnotes

[1] Booch, Grady. "The BCS/IET Manchester Turing Lecture." Manchester, 2007. http://intranet.cs.man.ac.uk/Events_subweb/special/turing07/.

[2] Splolsky, Joel. "Joel on Software." www.joelonsoftware.com/articles/LeakyAbstractions.html.

[3] Maier, Mark W. and Eberhardt Rechtin. *The Art of Systems Architecting.* CRC Press, Boca Raton, Florida, 2000.

[4] For example, IBM's Rational Tool Set.

7

Evolution of the Elephant Eater

"In the long history of humankind (and animal kind, too),
those who learned to collaborate and improvise most
effectively have prevailed."
—*Charles Darwin*

Chapter Contents

- The Sources of Brownfield   134
- Isn't This CASE?   138
- Isn't This MDA?   139
- Endnotes   142

The preceding chapters have explained the problems the industry faces when developing elephantine solutions. We have discussed the current development methods and highlighted their deficiencies. We have introduced the concepts and fundamental principles of Brownfield. We have also illustrated how its adoption can improve the current situations facing large-scale developments. Ultimately, Brownfield attempts to give the industry a method for reliable, large-scale IT development.

This chapter looks into the roots of Brownfield. We compare the technologies and methods that have aided in its development and thinking. We also illustrate the similarities and differences of the aspects these technologies and methods share with Brownfield.

The Sources of Brownfield

There's really no such thing as a completely new method. So-called new methods always build upon existing experiences and approaches, and often extend or continue the best practices of a number of them. Alternatively, new methods might repackage existing approaches or combine them in different ways. Again, Brownfield does not claim to be entirely new.

Brownfield took its inspiration from numerous disciplines. It is certainly not theoretical. Instead of being developed in a software product or research laboratory, it was actually conceived on real elephantine engagements in an attempt to resolve some of the many problems illustrated earlier in this book.

Far from trying to replace these existing disciplines, Brownfield utilizes many of them. Brownfield is really a different way of looking at the solution. It doesn't involve rushing in to write down the requirements, then develop and deliver a solution; it involves taking a deep breath first. It means surveying your existing environment, and taking time to understand and document it.

This enables you to view requirements in the context of that existing environment and understand the complexity involved. You can, thus, fully understand how the requirements relate to the complexity required to implement them. You can then model the implementations required and generate solutions. Repeating this through a number of iterations ultimately produces the final solution.

Numerous disciplines and practices helped inspire Brownfield:

- **Mashups**—The capability to quickly assemble an application that combines data or functionality from a number of sources.

- **Computer Aided Software Engineering (CASE)**—The use of software tools and a documented method to assist in the development and maintenance of software. The tools used are normally built around a single method and a proprietary repository. CASE, in general, takes little notice of the existing environment.

- **Computer Aided Design/Computer Aided Manufacturing (CAD/CAM)**—The ability to support multiple levels of abstraction, providing a graphical capability to visualize what is being designed. Advanced software enables physical artifacts to be produced directly from the drawing board.

- **Model Driven Architecture/Model Driven Development (MDA/MDD)**—The capability to generate solutions directly from computer models.

- **Rapid Application Development (RAD)**—A software-development process that uses iterative development and a flexible approach to usability, features, and execution speed. The result is the production of a solution in less time.

- **Joint Application Design/Development (JAD)**—Process of bringing together the people who will be using the system and the developers of the solution, to establish the requirements for the system in a dynamic and flexible manner.

- **Agile development methods**—An iterative development cycle in which a complete product is produced at the end of each iteration, even if it is not put into production. The emphasis of agile development is on working software rather than documentation.

- **Virtual worlds (v-worlds)**—A computer-based simulated environment that enables users to interact and visualize information in shared, often realistic, three-dimensional environments.

- **Semantic Web**—The next generation of Web technologies sponsored by Tim Berners-Lee (often regarded as the father of the World Wide Web). Web content can be expressed in both natural language and a more formal manner. This gives the information inherent, contextual meanings.

The rest of the book covers how Brownfield uses each of these techniques. However, Brownfield definitively isn't any of these capabilities or technologies alone. Table 7.1 summarizes how Brownfield makes use of these existing techniques and notes any differences between the standard forms of these techniques and Brownfield.

Table 7.1 Comparison Between Brownfield and More Established Techniques

Existing IT Technique	Similarities with Brownfield	Differences with Brownfield	Key Benefits of Technique	Key Drawbacks of Technique
Mashups	Capability to assemble solutions from existing implementations in a highly dynamic way.	Little support for legacy or existing capabilities.	Dynamic, low cost.	Little support for use of other people's code.
CASE	Imposed rigor, patterns, and structure that enable solutions to be generated.	Specific design methods and proprietary generation tools.	Rigor, speed, improved quality.	Many constraints imposed on the design and development. Heavy reliance on particular suppliers.
CAD/CAM	Capability to support multiple levels of abstraction and provide graphical ability to visualize the design. Software enables physical artifacts to be produced.	Currently used in the field of engineering rather than software engineering.	Automated drawing board to physical manufacture of solution.	Normally used for the basic building blocks of a solution.
MDA/MDD	Capability to generate solutions directly from models.	Models used as a proportion of the solution rather than a complete solution.	Fast, consistent, flexible. Maintainable solutions developed.	Model complexity limited by standards and tooling, especially around logic.
V-worlds	Emphasis on natural forms of communication using strong metaphors.	Complete visualization world and social network system.	Shared visualization with little overhead.	Can be insecure or too public for sensitive information.

Existing IT Technique	Similarities with Brownfield	Differences with Brownfield	Key Benefits of Technique	Key Drawbacks of Technique
Semantic Web	Relationship and documentation of information in a more formal manner.	Brownfield emphasizes the use of semantics technologies to engineer solutions as well as discover and classify information.	More formal capture of information.	Limited skills base and adoption of complex technologies; currently little perceived business value.
RAD/JAD	Iterative development and flexible approach to the establishment of requirements.	Development limited to small components. Informal capture of requirements.	Rapid development of solution in combination with the customer.	Limited use in large developments. No methods for integration.
Agile	Incremental and iterative approach.	Need for development to be broken into small units. Informal capture of requirements. Solutions that are written rather than generated.	Ever-improving solution with each iteration.	Limited use in large developments. No methods for integration.

Table 7.1 illustrates the modern technologies that underpin Brownfield. (Although, as stated earlier, Brownfield is more a change of philosophy than a specific set of technologies.)

Having briefly looked at the many disciplines that underpin Brownfield, we now examine two that provide the closest fit. We investigate CASE and MDA to see how they differ from Brownfield.

Isn't This CASE?

In the late 1980s and early 1990s, Computer Aided Software Engineering (CASE) tools were introduced. The goal of these tools was to automate software engineering, to help make software easier to develop and maintain. Unfortunately, the performance required from the hardware at that time meant that these tools tended to be slow and worked through nonintuitive interfaces. Instead of aiding the user's thought processes, often the opposite was true—the speed of the process hindered the user's creativity. These tools were limited to capturing the solution rather than becoming creative tools, and users often hated them.

Hardware performance has certainly improved since that time. Today's average PC is more than capable of providing the sort of power necessary for a high-speed, usable, graphical interface to manipulate data and is a much better basis for using CASE in today's solutions.

In the sense that a Brownfield solution is computer aided and certainly helps in software engineering, then, yes, it is CASE—but it is far more than this. Brownfield is more than software engineering. It extends up through process engineering, system engineering, project engineering, and even enterprise engineering. Brownfield builds upon the basis of CASE and extends it far beyond the original scope of CASE. Consider these key differences:

- CASE tools require that you use a particular method. Within Brownfield, the VITA process enables you to use a variety of design methods and tools. The results are then imported into the Inventory as Views.

- CASE tools typically use a proprietary repository to store the model. Brownfield's repository is the Inventory, which uses the open standards of RDF and OWL.

- CASE tools typically allow the automated generation of the code to a fixed pattern or framework. Code generation is the generation of the scripts that are executed to provide the required functionality. VITA and MDA support the generation of the code to configure patterns.

- CASE tools were not generally designed to allow post-generation modification—every time the application was generated, all hand-coded modifications had to be reapplied, often by hand. By generating the entire solution, VITA and MDA support a direct relationship between the requirements and the solution.

- CASE tools capture the solution, but not the existing environment where the solution is to be incorporated. CASE is fundamentally Greenfield in its approach.

In summary, Brownfield extends the basics of CASE and applied computer-aided techniques to generate complete solutions for problems that take the existing environment into account.

Isn't This MDA?

Model Driven Architecture (MDA) models a computer representation of the solution to help generate or produce Artifacts that are then used as a system (or part of a system). Certainly, a large part of Brownfield is the model-driven generation of solution Artifacts to build the solution. But this does not explain its full potential. MDA is normally used for small parts of the solution; it is not usually used on anything the size and scale of elephantine developments.

MDA and Brownfield both support the iterative discovery of requirements, though Brownfield formalizes this approach via the Site Survey. As additional requirements or constraints are discovered, they can be included in the model to generate a new solution. This is an important part of both MDA and Brownfield. Solutions will converge toward the required solution as more requirements and constraints are discovered and modeled.

Brownfield differs from MDA because it has no dependency on Unified Modeling Language (UML). The Views concept allows Brownfield to import all types of information in a variety of formats. This enables people to model in their own native language. According to the Object Management Group, an international open industry consortium that defines standards, the model in MDA must be written in UML. This goes against one of the Brownfield beliefs that people should be permitted to work in the modeling language in which they feel most comfortable. For this reason, Brownfield does not mandate the use of UML, although this is one of the modeling languages it supports.

Empowering the Business Analyst

In both MDA and Brownfield, business analysts (BAs) can undertake the modeling aspects. A high degree of rigor is required when using a model to generate solutions. This is greater than traditional methods necessarily enforce: Similar modeling might be used but often is accomplished using office type tooling. Although these models look similar, much more formality is required if the models are to be used for generation of solutions. This requires the BAs to increase the precision in producing the models, and experience shows that this is initially a problem. However, as soon as the BAs realize that what they are documenting and modeling defines the solution that is generated, they are willing to undertake the extra rigor in the modeling. With Brownfield, the solution can move closer to the business—it is driven now not by the programmers, but by the BAs.

MDA traditionally is used to define interfaces, screens, and even business processes, but each part of these would be based on a separate model. Brownfield has extended and merged these separate models into a single model: the Inventory. More than this, Brownfield builds on MDA in both the size and scope of the solution generated—but this is only one aspect of Brownfield.

Brownfield considers the complete solution and includes the original environment and its constraints in the Inventory. Brownfield uses visualization, described in Chapter 4, "The Trunk Road to the Brain," to convey the understanding of this model to the different groups of stakeholders. Instead of forcing these stakeholders to use a common tool or method (which would never work), Brownfield allows each stakeholder to use the tooling and method of their choice. This is then converted to a standard form when imported into the Inventory.

Brownfield can also be used in the testing of the solution. Essentially, this is performed in two stages. During the first stage, the generated system is automatically checked against the requirements that were used to generate it. This testing answers the question "Did we generate the system correctly?" The second testing stage checks that the system actually does what was intended. If the requirements used to generate the system were incomplete or incorrect, then these kinds of defects will be found via this second stage of tests. This stage normally involves the users of the system and is part of the enterprise's acceptance of the solution.

In the first stage of testing, verifying that the solution meets the requirements, Brownfield can be used to generate the required Artifacts to perform this testing, as the requirements are documented within the Inventory.

Brownfield also can generate the appropriate test scripts and test data, to accomplish the first stage of testing. Traditionally, this covers a major part of the testing that is required for solutions.

Of course, this is not the complete testing; the second stage tests that the solution performs as intended. Ideally, the requirements capture what was originally intended in the solution; however, this has not always been the case when using traditional Greenfield methods. Brownfield uses visualization and documentation in your own language to minimize this difference.

Thus, when the Brownfield solution is produced, it generally ends up doing what it was intended to do, as well as what it was specified to do.

Evolution, Not Revolution

This chapter has explained that Brownfield is not a revolutionary process. Instead, it has evolved from the best practices and most efficient disciplines within the industry today.

Brownfield brings a new way of looking at the problem. In any solution, best practice states that you document the problem and develop from that documented solution. Traditional Greenfield development methods fail to do this, for two reasons.

The first is that they do not take into account all the requirements. They fail to document the many constraints provided by the existing environment. Without these constraints, the requirements are incomplete. Unfortunately, traditional large-scale development methods are founded on the assumption that they have captured the complete set of requirements. Missing requirements are expensive to build into the solution at a late stage.

Second, the documentation is normally captured in an informal manner that does not force consistency. As a result, static testing (the manual inspection of the requirements and solution documentation) is used to try and detect any inconsistencies. This is a time-consuming and imprecise process—if it is done at all. In cases of poor Greenfield practice, this type of testing is often omitted in favor of simple, independent documentation reviews.

In contrast, Brownfield uses the site survey to resolve both of these by capturing the constraints in a more formal and consistent manner: within the Inventory. This Inventory builds on the semantic Web technologies that exist today. Even though the Brownfield process is designed to capture more of the requirements at the start of the process, it can also cope with incomplete requirements. As each iteration of the Brownfield process is performed, the requirements—and, hence, the solution—are made more complete.

On top of this strong foundation, Brownfield combines and extends many traditional and new disciplines to provide a complete solution.

Generated visualization from virtual worlds confirms and describes the solution to all concerned. MDD, agile, and RAD techniques are combined to provide an iterative and controlled development approach. This is brought together in a solution that supports the development and creation of large-scale incrementally reengineered IT solutions in complex environments.

Brownfield brings together and extends all these disciplines to build the ultimate Elephant Eater. The next chapter looks at how such an Elephant Eater is constructed.

Endnotes

Berners-Lee, Tim, James Hendler, and Ora Lissila. "The Semantic Web." *Scientific American*, Volume 284, No. 5 (May 2001): 29–35.

Mercurio, V.J., B.F. Meyers, A.M. Nisbit, and G. Radin. "AD/Cycle® Strategy and Architecture." *IBM Systems Journal*, Volume 29, No. 2 (1990): 171–188.

Mukerji, Jishnu and Joaquin Miller, eds. *MDA Guide V1.0.1: Overview and Guide to OMG's Architecture.* www.omg.org, June 2003.

Wood, Jane and Denise Silver. *Joint Application Development.* John Wiley & Sons, 1995.

8

Brownfield Development

"The process of scientific discovery is, in effect, a continual flight from wonder."
—*Albert Einstein*

Chapter Contents

- Agile Waterfalls   144
- The Brownfield Development Approach   158
- Endnotes   163

The previous chapter discussed the methods and techniques that form the foundations of Brownfield. We investigated each of these and compared the differences and similarities. Brownfield was shown to have evolved from these methods.

This chapter shows how the Brownfield method is used within the project lifecycle. As in the previous chapter, the lifecycle approach has again evolved as a composite of a number of existing lifecycle approaches.

Agile Waterfalls

Large-scale development has traditionally been based around well-organized phases. Each phase is completed before moving on to the next phase and is defined through work breakdown structures, work product definitions, and quality criteria. When viewed on a plan, these phases form steps down the page; this picture has led to the term "waterfall development." The water moves in only one direction, filling each phase before moving on to the next phase.

The more complex projects get, the more rigorous the methods become—up to and including extensive use of static testing[1] and formal systems engineering techniques. These techniques are used to form quality assurance checkpoints at key points along the waterfall. The checkpoints check progress and create rigorous, strong baselines. The baselines are made up of a single set of unambiguous, formally signed-off documents. Figure 8.1 shows these project phases together with the quality assurance checkpoints used to enforce the rigor. The example shown uses the baselines defined in Carnegie Mellon's Software Engineering Institute's Capability Maturity Model® Integration (CMMI®).

On very large projects, many people have tried to shortcut this process (deliberately or through ineptitude, or both), and many have come unstuck.

As Barry Boehm and Richard Turner point out in their book, *Balancing Agility and Discipline: A Guide for the Perplexed*,[2] five factors determine whether waterfall or agile methods will prevail on any particular project. For the purposes of this book, we have rephrased them, but we have stayed true to the spirit of their findings (see Table 8.1).

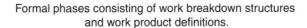

Formal phases consisting of work breakdown structures
and work product definitions.

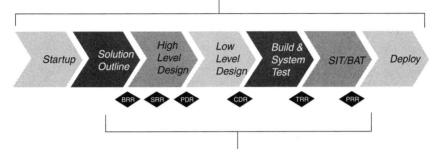

Baseline gates during or at the end of phases
specify what work product must be complete
with specific quality criteria.

Figure 8.1   The major phases of the waterfall lifecycle are punctuated by formal gates that allow baselines (often commercial ones) to be defined.

Table 8.1   Comparison of Agile and Waterfall Methods

Factor	Agile Characteristics	Waterfall Characteristics
Size	Optimal for small projects and teams; reliance on tacit knowledge	Tailored for large projects and teams
Mission-critical projects	Untested; general lack of documentation	Long history of use in such implementations
Stability and complexity of existing environment	Continuous refactoring used; suitable for dynamic and simple environments (typically Greenfield)	Structured baselines used; suitable for more static and complex environments (typically Brownfield)
Skills	Continuous involvement of highly skilled individuals; difficult to cope with many lower skilled resources	Highly skilled individuals needed in early phases; designed to cope with many lower-skilled resources in later phases
Suitable organization culture	Chaotic; dynamic; empowered	Roles well defined; procedures in place

As you can see, agile and waterfall development each have their strengths and drawbacks. To recast the comparison, it is both possible and safe to build a paper airplane without a detailed plan. It would be foolish to spend 20 minutes writing the instructions and then spend 20 seconds building the plane. However, building a passenger airliner without detailed, upfront design would be a long and expensive process involving a *lot* of rework that you would otherwise have avoided. (You'd also probably face a shortage of test pilots to take the airliner on its maiden flight.) Figure 8.2 summarizes the different development techniques used in building a paper airplane and building an airliner.

Rapid	Slow
Iterative	Waterfall
Little Documentation	Lots of Documentation
Rework Is Cost Effective	Rework Is Expensive

Figure 8.2 The development techniques used for a paper airplane and an airliner should be quite different.

In formal waterfall methods, defects are detected as early as possible through static and then executable testing. If defects are found, changes are made to the requirements, specifications, or solution design documents. Changes can ripple forward from the first work product affected to the last. This approach reduces the overall number of defects and is far more cost-effective than not following these best practices because it reduces the number of surprises and the amount of rework.

Stringent baselines and static testing of work products improves overall quality and helps ensure that more defects are found earlier. However, this is not a cheap method of delivering systems. A high level of process and discipline is required, and the method does not take into account the complexity of the environment much more than any other Greenfield method. The knowledge and impact of those thousands of constraints is still held over to the end of the project, typically into the late testing phases when changes are expensive, even with the best possible walkthroughs and inspections.

In reality, even in rigorous projects, a detailed requirement fault detected late in the waterfall lifecycle generally does not result in a change to the original requirements and demand that the subsequent work products and baselines be re-created and revalidated. Generally, workarounds for such problems are found and the proper solution is postponed to the next release.

Traditional waterfall methods decompose the problem to ever-smaller Views until the View is sufficiently small, detailed, and self-contained for it to be built by an individual, often in isolation. These Views are then tested in the reverse order of the decomposition, up to the final stage of a complete acceptance test. Unfortunately, this encourages a testing of the system by Views, too. Some of those Views (such as the integration or data migration elements) are often tested late and are expensive to fix. As you learned earlier in this book, it's cheaper to fix things at the front of the process. Figure 8.3 shows the decomposition and testing of the views together with the increased cost of finding an error in that phase.

Cost to Remove Defect

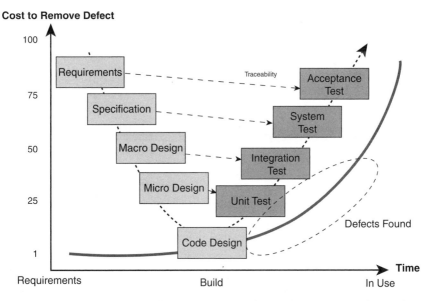

Figure 8.3   The cost of removing a defect increases exponentially as time progresses; unfortunately, the industry "best practice" test model encourages late testing of some areas of high uncertainty (such as integration).

This test model, known as the V model because of its shape, is currently the industry's best practice, but the requirements testing is performed only at the latest stage of the project lifecycle. This is the most expensive point in a project to find such errors and undoubtedly causes delays in what seemed like a project that was on schedule. Surely, a more cost-effective way of testing would be to follow the approach shown in Figure 8.4.

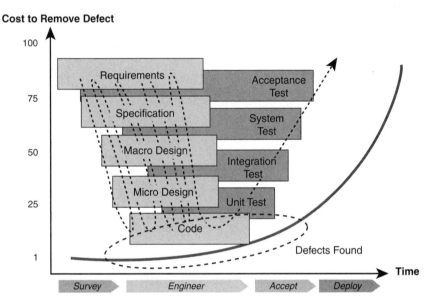

Figure 8.4 An iterative approach that dives deep through the testing procedures would encourage earlier testing and cheaper defect removal. The difficulty with this approach, however, is that it requires an agile approach, which could also work with highly complex, heavily constrained designs.

This alternative model preserves the traceability of the original testing model, but the testing of the corresponding baseline is performed as soon as possible. In addition, "deep dives" are repeatedly made by building some aspects of the system early and testing them against the requirements; this enables at least some of the late-stage testing to be brought forward. This approach clearly looks a lot like agile[3] development, and it is—agile works by effectively implementing some of the requirements and then using this to capture further requirements as deltas for the current situation. This is repeated until the total requirements are captured.

Unfortunately, the agile approach works well only for Greenfield projects or medium-size projects in simple environments; the approach is often flawed for bigger, more complex solutions or those that have a lot of constraints. The previous chapter detailed an example of a Greenfield approach destroying an essentially Brownfield project with the creation of a Web front end on a complex credit card processing legacy system. In that particular project, agile techniques were used to determine the user interface and Domain Object Model (DOM) that formed the basis of the new system. The DOM defined the business information and structures used to define the problem, and these were developed iteratively with the business. Alongside the DOM, user interface prototypes and object models were iteratively refined based on business user feedback.

However, the constraints of the legacy system were poorly understood, and the DOM that was created was inherently incompatible with its surrounding environment. The iterative approach did not allow those elements to be properly understood early enough.

Waterfall techniques are excellent at dealing with the nonfunctionals, good at dealing with functionals, and reasonably good at dealing with constraints. Agile is excellent with the functionals, poor with nonfunctionals, and very poor with constraints.

The options for a sizeable reengineering project seem to boil down to these:

- Finding out all the requirements, including constraints, before starting, and designing the ideal system to implement them (very expensive)

- Growing the solution and discovering all the requirements as you go, but with the effect of building a suboptimal system and the danger of substantial rework (also very expensive)

We need a technique that combines the best bits of agile and waterfall but that sorts out how to handle constraints. What has the industry achieved in this space so far?

Agility under Waterfalls, or Waterfalls with Agility?

Boehm and Turner look at good examples of hybrid waterfall/agile approaches in their book *Balancing Agility and Discipline.* One example takes a look at an agile project of considerable size and another considerably sized, mission-critical project with agile-like deadlines and targets that demand agile behavior.

Looking at a successful project that used agile programming techniques to deliver a system of the magnitude we are talking about, Boehm and Turner found the following to be true:

- The effort to deliver features increased nonlinearly over time (well outside the bounds of a normal agile project). As you might expect from earlier chapters of this book, this was ascribed mostly to communications overheads.

- Increased formality was required around the design. Architectural perspectives were required to divide work and to ensure a valid design for areas that were both complex and subject to change.

- Tacit knowledge was not enough to define all the requirements (especially for specialized use of complex function) and did not scale sufficiently.

- An "integration" gap (of some 12 weeks) arose between "zero defect" functionally "complete" code and actual delivery of working integrated code.

As a result, some of the key tenets of agile programming had to be diluted or lost completely from their hybrid approach. These findings strongly match our experience in using agile techniques on large projects.

Using another example in the same book, we look at a fundamentally waterfall-created, mission-critical system that applied agile techniques to accelerate its development. Boehm and Turner noted that agile development on its own was not enough to maintain control, and they had to introduce the following innovations:

- The documentation for the system needed to be automatically generated from the architecture and code artifacts.

- The early phases of the project were used to design and develop robust patterns that could underpin the elements developed with agility.

- Integration and performance testing was performed early and often instead of being performed at the end.

Both of these examples are telling. The three points mentioned are also techniques we have used on Brownfield projects. Certainly, we should expect any "hybrid" method that contains the best of agile and waterfall to offer the kind of capabilities identified in the previous best practices examples. We believe that the Brownfield approach enshrines such a method that enables all three kinds of requirements (functional, nonfunctional, and constraints) to be applied iteratively and incrementally throughout a project without losing control.

Let's look at a specific example of what the Brownfield approach is capable of—and let's choose a painful example for traditional waterfall *or* agile approaches: the integration of a new system with a highly complex, mission-critical legacy system. Both methods tend to fall down in this area: Waterfall tends to find defects late; agile tends not to apply constraints early enough.

An Agile Approach to a Waterfall Problem

Determining all the requirements of an interface is often difficult, especially when dealing with a legacy interface. This is why so many large system projects stall at integration testing. An agile-type development style on interfaces might seem the ideal solution, but it is difficult to discover the requirements, and current approaches fail to turn around solutions fast enough to uncover a solution to missing requirements (usually constraints).

Capturing interface requirements relies on many stages of copying and translation before implementation. This creates a whispering game, which can be countered only by additional effort in cross-checking. A large part of the cost of testing an interface is in verifying that the built interface actually performs as specified. This normally has to happen before any real testing of an interface can be performed.

The whole situation is then made worse by assuming that the world stops when the project starts—that is, that requirements are captured at a point in time and don't change. Is this a realistic assumption?

Clearly, when existing and well-established systems are involved in the integration, their release cycle is unlikely to synchronize with that of any new project. The constraints on the interface might subtly or importantly change during the elapsed time of the change project. Indeed, with the high stack of paper that described the interface constraints on one of our projects, it would have been surprising if a significant number of those pages hadn't changed over the duration of a big project.

Surely there must be a better way.

These kinds of problems led to the development of the Brownfield approach.

Turning Model Driven Architecture on Its Head

So, how is this achieved?

The Brownfield development approach is partly based on the Model Driven Architecture (MDA) approach. Brownfield development extends

MDA with the VITA architecture that Chapter 3, "Big-Mouthed Superhero Required," introduced.

MDA is defined by the Open Management Group (OMG) as a way to enhance the delivery of systems so that a description of the business problem can be created independent of any specific technology.[4]

The industry has been on a long journey since before *The Mythical Man Month* to create standards for the formal documentation of its designs and its code. As you learned in Chapter 6, "Abstraction Works Only in a Perfect World," there has also been a gradual rise of the abstraction level of code itself during this time (from machine code to business-modeling tools and the like).

Typically, these days this means that the models developers use to describe the code also work for round-trip engineering. The picture-based models are used to generate code "stubs," which the developer must then fill in. If the developer changes the code so that the model needs to be updated, the model will be automatically updated as a result (hence, "round-trip").

MDA takes this stub approach a step further and makes the model the central part of the process, with significant elements of the code being automatically generated from yet more abstract-level models.

Within the MDA philosophy are important divisions between the model types, creating a spectrum from business through to technology. These models are the Computation Independent Model (CIM), the Platform Independent Model (PIM), and the Platform Specific Model (PSM, which is then characterized by a Platform Model).

Table 8.2 describes the major characteristics of these models:

Table 8.2 Major Models in Model Driven Architecture

Model	Description
Computation Independent Model (CIM)	A CIM does not portray any structure of the system that supports it. More colloquially, this is known as the Domain Model. Terminology that is familiar to the business itself gives it a way to represent the structure of the business problem.
Platform Independent Model (PIM)	The PIM is a representation of the system without the specification of any technology. This is more colloquially known as the logical or analysis-level model.
Platform Specific Model (PSM)	The PSM specifies how the PIM is implemented on a particular platform. Typically, the PSM is expressed via the relationship between the PIM and a Platform Model (PM). (For often-used platforms such as CORBA or J2EE, Platform Models are already available.)

Figure 8.5 shows how these models are used to generate code that is relevant to the business problem (described in the domain).

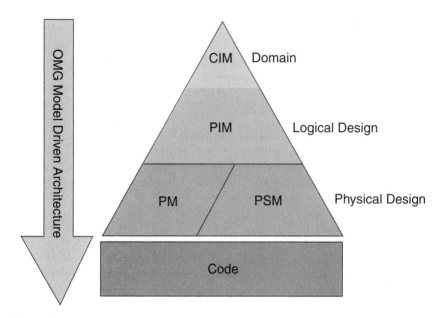

Figure 8.5   The major phases and models of the OMG MDA approach

This layering approach enables you to make the implementation choice (described by the PSM) of a particular business problem later in the project lifecycle. It also enhances the capability to move solutions between implementation platforms—or even to implement them on more than one platform, if necessary.

Pattern Driven Engineering

Pattern Driven Engineering (PDE) extends the MDA approach by encouraging the adoption of industry-proven patterns at each stage of the modeling process. These might be existing domain models (such as the IBM Insurance Application Architecture model for the insurance industry[5] that operates at all the modeling layers of the MDA stack) or simply well-recognized patterns specific to a particular technology. IBM has recently begun to formally identify and classify patterns that assist in the transformation of existing environments. (Aptly, these are informally known as Brownfield patterns.)

PDE is not yet as well known as MDA, but it likely will underpin the next wave of enterprise solutions, architectures, and assets. Such use of patterns improves the maintainability, understandability, and reusability. In addition, because these are proven patterns, they should maximize the future flexibility of the generated systems. Patterns are a key mechanism to accelerate design and implementation while minimizing risk as they are previously proven and considered "best practice."

Model Driving Is Not a One-Way Street

Brownfield was born out of projects that made extensive use of MDA and early use of PDE to solve complex business problems. Brownfield, however, takes things a significant step further.

Brownfield builds on this MDA/PDE process of increasing precision and reducing abstraction *by reversing it.*

Brownfield uses code from your existing environment, code patterns, application patterns, and architectural patterns to infer the existence of the CIM.

Instead of applying patterns in a structured way, we identify the key patterns used at each layer of the existing environment and represent the environment at gradually higher levels of abstraction. Step by step, the underlying structure and logic from the existing environment is reverse-engineered. In simple environments with many existing sources of formal documentation, this is a quick process. In more complex, undocumented, or badly designed or architected environments, this can take much longer. In general, it is not cost-effective to understand *everything* about an environment, but to focus in on those areas that are central to understanding the problem being worked on.

Ultimately, the technology-independent elements that describe the existing business implementation can be represented in the Inventory. With the existing business problem so defined, the reengineering of the domain, logical, or physical system can be performed. This reengineering, which is performed by the creation and manipulation of target Views, often models themselves, can now be done in the full knowledge of the existing constraints that the existing systems impose. This enables us to impose a real-life understanding of the impact of any proposed changes.

The reengineering process then becomes an iterative one, with new Artifacts describing the new solution. These Artifacts can be modified models, new run-time elements, or simply visualizations of the new elements in context.

We can then use the existing MDA/PDE process outlined earlier to regenerate and reengineer elements of the business problem. Figure 8.6 shows a comparison with the MDA approach.

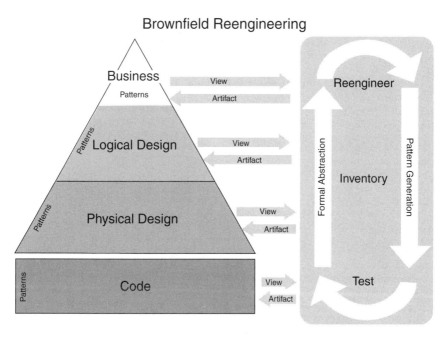

Figure 8.6 Brownfield development turns MDA on its head by identifying patterns in Views, inferring the architecture from them, and then using more patterns to generate the solution.

We likely will not get the CIM from the code in one step, so the process is one of gradual refinement and incremental understanding—but it is fundamentally automated and much faster than trying to find out the information using conventional interview techniques or code inspections. Each time the Views are fed into the Inventory, additional observed patterns that were identified as missing from the previous iteration are fed into its "vocabulary" for conversion into Inventory entries.

As the code and architectural layering of the system are identified, the high-level, business logic elements of the system become more obvious as they are separated from the middleware or infrastructure code. The process is fast but necessarily incremental: It may initially be impossible to see the wood for the trees, but after a number of iterations, the areas of interest for the logical and business layers of the solution become clearer. The platform-specific elements are identified and fed into the Inventory, enabling the higher-level structures to be inferred or harvested.

Brownfield Encourages Earlier Testing

The speed and efficiency of harvesting is further enhanced by the use of the Inventory to generate interim Artifacts that can be used for testing purposes.

These Artifacts can be documents, visualizations, or actual executables. Documents and visualizations are used for static testing. In static testing, the final solution is not available to be executed, so other techniques, such as walkthroughs, inspections, or mappings, are used to detect incompleteness or defects.

With an Inventory, the static testing mapping technique becomes highly automated. The Inventory is particularly powerful when the definition of one poorly understood element of a problem has to match a well-understood area. Missing Inventory entries (missing mappings or missing equivalent data in source and target, for example) are obvious clues for missing requirements and constraints.

The capability of Brownfield to cope with partial information over multiple iterations means that even executable testing becomes possible, potentially earlier in the lifecycle than would otherwise be the case. Not only that, but the quick cycle time of the Brownfield process means that iterative testing and improvement becomes the preferred way to work.

Accelerated Delivery on a Brownfield Site

In a previous project, the Inventory was used to generate interface Artifacts for a complex environment. Now, when the project began, certain key elements of the environment were not known. First, the legacy systems that the interface had to connect to were unknown entities. Second, the executable environment for the interfaces was an Enterprise Service Bus (ESB) that had not yet been defined.

Although the project had access to basic interface specifications that described the format of messages and their valid content, the interface specifications did not contain all the information about the internal constraints of the legacy systems that governed their behavior. This information was not forthcoming because no one knew what it was.

In addition, although the team knew the basic patterns involved in creating a generic ESB, it was unclear which directions some of the key architectural decisions would go. Prevailing wisdom would have said, "Don't write any code until you know how the ESB is going to be built."

A Brownfield analysis of the major areas of the target legacy system code was a possibility, but access to the code was less than straightforward. As a result, the team decided to use a Brownfield approach to iteratively generate simple interfaces that could be enhanced over time.

The generation process did not just create pattern-based implementations of the necessary interfaces; it also generated (via an independent generation process) test cases that could help determine whether the Artifacts—and their generation process—were working as expected. This automation largely removed the need for unit and component system testing.

As failures from the automated tests were collected, the reasons for the failures were captured and used to augment the knowledge collected about the business domain. This new business domain knowledge was used to regenerate the interfaces, and the testing was repeated.

Simultaneously, as aspects of the ESB implementation became clearer, the patterns used to generate the interface implementations were enhanced to look more like the target platform model. Initially, the implementation was point to point (shown at the top of the diagram in Figure 8.7). Over a series of iterations, as the architecture of the ESB solution was decided and formal documentation was issued, the complexity of the model-driven implementation increased until the final solution included all the necessary patterns for a full-fledged and resilient ESB with redundancy across two sites.

The iterative approach allowed a much earlier and much more gradual improvement of the logical correctness and completeness of the interface definition (the business definition) because the failure conditions were analyzed from the early model-driven implementations. If we had let the project wait until the final shape of the ESB was defined and had only discovered the unknown elements within the legacy systems when undertaking integration testing, then many months would have been added to the duration of the project. With more than 100 highly skilled people on the project, that's conservatively a saving of $10 million.

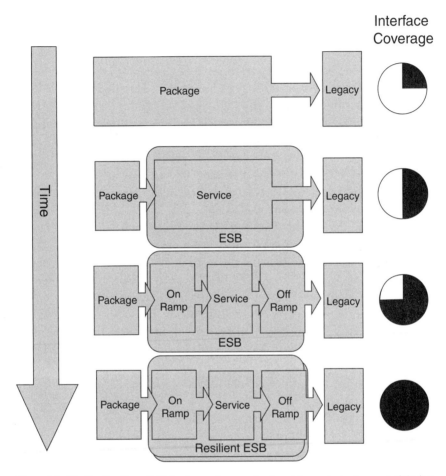

Figure 8.7 The iterative Brownfield development approach allowed the gradual refinement of the logical and physical architectures and incremental testing for the whole approach, resulting in earlier and cheaper defect removal.

The Brownfield Development Approach

From the previous description, you can more clearly see how the Brownfield techniques can accelerate and improve the solution quality of difficult and complex projects. Figure 8.8 summarizes the Brownfield development approach.

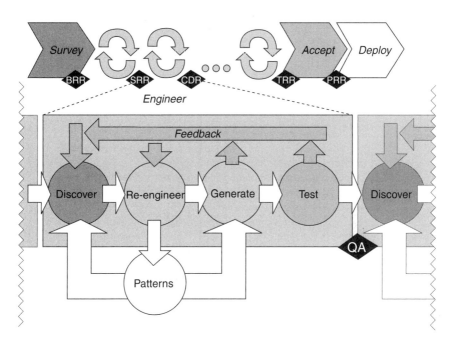

Figure 8.8   The Brownfield development approach has four key phases, with the main Engineering Phase being highly iterative.

Brownfield essentially takes an iterative approach for design, development, and much of testing (in line with the modified V model we showed earlier). The main sequence of the method is essentially waterfall, however, and is split conventionally into four phases, as shown in Figure 8.8 and Table 8.3.

Table 8.3   Major Phases and Outputs of Brownfield Development Approach

Phase	Description	Major Outputs
Survey	During the Survey Phase, the boundary of the solution is determined via a business context and a gathering of business events. The environment is scoured for potential inputs that lie within that boundary or interact over it. These inputs form part of a site survey, which is fed into the Inventory. The phase ends with an engineering plan being created, which structures the iterative engineering cycle that follows.	Business context Business events Use case list Inventory Engineering plan

Table 8.3   Major Phases and Outputs of Brownfield Development Approach (continued)

Phase	Description	Major Outputs
Engineering	The Engineering Phase is executed at least three times, but should ideally be executed on a daily to weekly cycle. (On a large project, it might be executed more than 100 times.) It follows a process of discovery, engineering, generation, and testing with feedback within that process. During this phase, the description of the problem, the solution, and the patterns underpinning the solution are incrementally refined. The individual steps within the Engineering Phase are covered in more detail later in this chapter. A formal estimation of project size (based on the Inventory, use case list, and problem definition) should be used to determine the actual cycle numbers and dates for n_1, n_2, n_{last} at the end of the Survey Phase and then should be revised at the end of Iteration n_1. The Engineering Phase finalizes the Problem Definition and Solution Definition.	**Iteration #n_1 (SRR)** Systems context Use cases Problem definition (CIM) **Iteration #n_2** **(CDR)** PIM definition Component model Operational model Performance model Source code Executables Test specifications Test report **Iteration #n_{last}** **(TRR)** PSM definition Test report Deployment package
Accept	This phase performs the formal acceptance of the system by completing any remaining testing. The focus should be on acceptance and operational testing because other areas should be complete.	Test report Education and training materials
Deploy	The accepted solution is handed over to service delivery and application maintenance personnel. Training and education for the new solution commences. The solution goes live.	Application maintenance turnover package Service delivery turnover package

The Engineering Phase is worthy of specific attention because it breaks down into a number of subphases. The Engineering Phase is iterative in two ways; first, it is run at least three times during an engagement; in addition, it has built-in iterative feedback mechanisms within the phase itself. Table 8.4 describes the Engineering Phase.

Table 8.4 The Subphases and Outputs of the Brownfield Engineering Phase

Subphase	Description	Major Outputs
Discovery	The Discovery phase is where additional information is fed into the Inventory. This information is in the form of formal Views or existing assets from the surrounding environment. Additional patterns can be created or sought out in this phase to increase the depth or breadth of knowledge within the Inventory.	Inventory updates Problem definition updates
Reengineering	Within the Reengineering Phase, the knowledge in the Inventory forms the basis for a highly detailed description of the problem and, increasingly, a detailed description of the solution. It is likely that the "to be" state is different from the "as is," and so some reengineering of Views, often expressed as models, is necessary. A pattern, asset, or package also might need to be reengineered to provide a good fit to the solution. Feedback from earlier engineering cycles will need to be taken into account in the solution definition and pattern definitions.	Definition updates Modified patterns Transforms
Generate	The Inventory and patterns are combined to generate the solution or test Artifacts. Test Artifacts can include design documentation or visualizations for walkthroughs, formal test specifications, or unit test cases for executable testing. The generation component (also known as a Factory) can identify generation faults (which are corrected locally) or missing Inventory information that requires feedback to the next Discovery phase.	Factory defects (resolved locally for next iteration) View defects (fed into next Discovery iteration) Design documentation Visualizations Test specifications Unit test cases

Table 8.4   The Subphases and Outputs of the Brownfield Engineering Phase (continued)

Subphase	Description	Major Outputs
Test	Within each engineering iteration, some static or executable testing must be performed. Such tests will result in feedback for the correction of Views that are missing information (Discovery) or Views that need to be updated (Reengineering).	Test reports View defects (fed into next Discovery iteration)

This chapter described how the Brownfield lifecycle is undertaken on a project. The lifecycle differs from that of the traditional waterfall method employed on large-scale developments and instead utilizes a more agile approach to the development lifecycle.

This approach has four major phases per release: the Survey, Engineering, Accept, and Deploy phases.

Within the Survey Phase is a site survey, just like what would be undertaken when building. The constraints of the existing environment are captured and then fed into the Inventory for later use.

The Engineering Phase is the main development phase on the project; it contains an iterative process of discovery, reengineering, generation, and testing. Requirements are discovered and introduced into the Inventory. The Inventory can them be checked to assess the implications of these requirements against the constraints captured during the survey phase. Reengineering includes the modeling of the problem and the application of patterns. The solution is then generated and tested. This cycle is repeated until the solution is complete.

The Acceptance Phase is the formal customer acceptance of the system. This includes operational and acceptance testing.

The final phase is to Deploy the solution, including handing it over to the operational staff, and to provide any training and education required to operate the system.

All these combine in a simple manner within a process to develop a large-scale development project efficiently while still retaining control of the project. Now that you understand the overall Brownfield process, the next chapter looks under the covers of the tooling that is required to support this process.

Endnotes

[1] Static testing consists of techniques such as inspections and design walk-throughs to test the system's requirements, design, and implementation before the system can be executed.

[2] Boehm, Barry and Richard Turner. *Balancing Agility and Discipline: A Guide for the Perplexed.* Boston, MA: Addison-Wesley, 2004.

[3] This can equally be attributed to Rapid Application Development (RAD). Agile is used in this case as the current best practice of RAD-type development.

[4] Mukerji, Jishnu and Joaquin Miller, eds. *MDA Guide V1.0.1, Overview and Guide to OMG's Architecture.* www.omg.org/docs/omg/03-06-01.pdf.

[5] IBM Financial Services Solutions. "Insurance Application Architecture." www-03.ibm.com/industries/financialservices/doc/content/solution/278918103.html.

9

Inside the Elephant Eater

"We shall not fail or falter; we shall not waste or tire....
Give us the tools and we shall finish the job."
—*Winston Churchill*

Chapter Contents

- Looking Inside the Elephant Eater   166
- Step 1: Parse View and Identify Patterns   169
- Step 2: Merge Views   183
- Step 3: Create Transforms   197
- Step 4: Generate Artifacts   198
- Steps 5.1: Test Artifacts and 5.1a: Identify Generation Faults   199
- Step 5.1b: Add and Update Information   199
- A Portrait of an Elephant Eater   200
- Endnotes   201

Chapter 3, "Big-Mouthed Superhero Required," explained how the Elephant Eater was structured via the VITA architecture. Views are combined and interlinked in a single Inventory that can contain much of the aggregated knowledge of the existing environment and ways of working.

This Inventory supports translation between different representations of the same concept (Transforms) so that the enterprise can be pulled together into a documented baseline of understanding—a single source of truth. The Inventory can then be sliced from any perspective to generate Artifacts that can help engineer a solution to the problem.

Because the Artifacts are created from the Inventory, we can be sure that they will correctly represent the environment around them and will be consistent.

The machinery to support this capability is called the Elephant Eater. The overarching approach is called the Brownfield development approach. The terms Brownfield and Elephant Eater are used because the approach and tooling are designed to deliver large reengineering projects in existing complex business and IT environments.

This chapter delves into what is inside the Elephant Eater and explores some technologies and techniques that make it possible to build an Elephant Eater.

Looking Inside the Elephant Eater

Clearly, the flow of the Brownfield development approach differs significantly from conventional large-scale IT systems development approaches. The approach is possible only when underpinned by the appropriate tooling. This chapter expands upon the Engineering subphase described in the previous chapter and looks at how Brownfield VITA-based tooling supports it.

Figure 9.1 provides further information on the Brownfield technology operation, expressed in terms of the VITA architecture presented in Chapter 3.

Views can be any means of describing the problem that follows a structured format. In practice, this is the Data Definition Language (DDL), use case, schemas, component models, process models, component business models, and even code. The following pages walk through Figure 9.1, following the steps and explaining how each element of the Elephant Eater works.

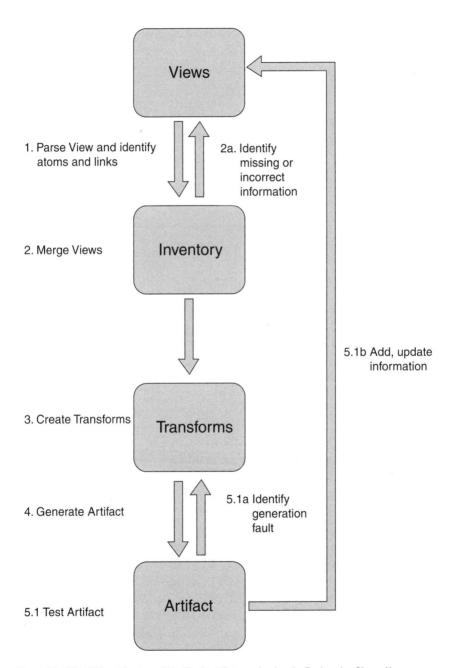

Figure 9.1   The VITA architecture of the Elephant Eater underpins the Engineering Phase. You can see the detailed flow of information around the Elephant Eater.

Views can be built from a wide variety of sources. Moving development tooling away from proprietary configurations to more open and published standards is helping the cause of Brownfield enormously. For example, Eclipse is an open-source community creating an open development platform. All Eclipse-based tools can easily be harvested to form part of an Inventory by creating plug-ins to facilitate the input the Inventory needs.

Table 9.1 lists other data sources that have been successfully harvested to form Inventories.

Table 9.1 Examples of View Input Types

Data Format	Harvested Examples
Spreadsheets	Service models, requirements traceability and verification matrixes, nonfunctional requirements
UML	Class diagrams, sequence diagrams, activity diagrams from component models and service component models
XML/RDF/OWL	Other ontologies and inventories, including infrastructure inventories
Formal data definitions	DDL and SQL, enabling the import of database schemas WSDL and XML Schema for Web services
Code	Legacy COBOL, C++, Java, HTML

We forecast that, over the next 10 years, the availability of discovery and static analysis tools will increase as clients demand flexibility from their existing estates instead of replacing them with new Greenfield applications. This will be the birth of the Brownfield movement, as the discovered information is drawn together in Inventories to enable reengineering and greater maintainability.

An early example of Brownfield discovery tooling is Tivoli® Application Dependency Discovery Manager (TADDM). TADDM can automatically discover the application infrastructure landscape of complex sites, including the layout of custom-developed applications built on J2EE or .NET.

The process of pulling together all these sources of information is collectively called the site survey. As in the rest of Brownfield, the site survey takes its name from the construction industry. If you wanted to build on any Brownfield site, local legislation would always insist that you do a thorough site survey first. We suggest that IT should be no different. The Brownfield development approach provides a cost-effective way of performing the site survey.

After you find and assemble the required Views, you must parse them into the Inventory.

Step 1: Parse View and Identify Patterns

Sometimes parsing a View is straightforward. Sometimes a View is simply created in a spreadsheet to stitch together two other previously unrelated Views. In such cases, the View is nothing more than a list of elements from View A paired with related elements from View B.

Diagrammatic views (such as UML diagrams) are not much harder. The Brownfield team has created an exporter that can automatically translate UML diagrams into simple subject/verb/object sentences that the Inventory uses. (*Predicate* is more formally used instead of *verb* in this context.) Using a class diagram as an example, the classes become subjects or objects, and the associations between those classes become verbs. Associations in UML are bidirectional by default, so a single association can often become two subject/verb/object sentences. These simple sentences are known as triples because they involve three elements. (The more correct term is *semantic triple.*)

In the simple example that follows, a small extract is provided from a component model. This component model describes the logical design of a small part of a system. Figure 9.2 shows how two components of the system talk to each other.

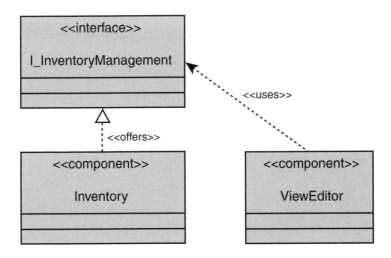

Figure 9.2 The two components shown talk to each other via an interface.

Don't worry about the exact meaning of the lines and << >> symbols. For someone who understands UML, these lines make things clearer, but you don't need to understand them; a textual description of the diagram will suffice to explain the point: In Figure 9.2, the Inventory is providing an interface that enables other components to interact with it (such as, submit data for inclusion). The diagram shows that such a View editing program (perhaps a spreadsheet) can use the advertised interface to talk to the Inventory. This diagram would be exported to the Inventory as a series of triples (see Table 9.2).

Table 9.2   Translation of Figure 9.2 into Triples

Subject	Verb	Object
Inventory	Offers	I_InventoryManagement
I_InventoryManagement	isOfferedBy	Inventory
ViewEditor	Uses	I_InventoryManagement
I_InventoryManagement	isUsedBy	ViewEditor

Harvesting a Brownfield

Thus, it is easy to understand how such formal diagrams, XML, or spreadsheets can become Views. But for Brownfield to be truly effective, it must be capable of processing even the most mysterious of formal forms: legacy code (usually COBOL).

Now, this would be an almost impossible task if computer languages were not (by necessity) formally defined. Their formal definition puts them into exactly the right structure for them to be fed into our Inventory.

This is because the syntax (formal structure) of any computer language is almost always described (except for XML) in a variant of a standard form called the Backus–Naur Form (BNF). This syntax definition language was invented in the 1960s by John Backus to define ALGOL and then was simplified by Peter Naur.

When a program is parsed to be compiled, these BNF definitions are used to define a tree structure that can describe any valid program in that particular language. These Abstract Syntax Trees (ASTs) are routinely used throughout the computer industry to create development tools.

When a developer today uses advanced editing features within a code-editing program (such as when the editor automatically anticipates what is needed to finish a line of code), the development program is probably not analyzing the source code directly. More commonly, the code editor has loaded the developer's code into an AST. The editing program then can conveniently analyze and modify the program source, ensuring that it remains consistent with the language definition.

As a result, programs to create ASTs from code have been readily available for pretty much any formal language since the 1960s. Some programs even use the formal BNF syntax definitions to automatically create programs that will read your programs and create the ASTs for you.

For the skeptical, Listing 9.1 gives a quick example of a simple Java™ program. The program simply declares a string called message with the content "Hello World" and then displays that message on the computer screen.

Listing 9.1   "Hello World" in Java

```
public class AstExample {
    public static void main(String[] args) {
        String message = "Hello World";
        System.out.println(message);
    }
}
```

This short program was written within the Java editor that is available within Eclipse. Eclipse is a freely available open-source editor (www.eclipse.org). Eclipse sees this source code in a structure similar to our subjects, verbs, and objects. For each method, variable declaration, assignment of a value, or any other major valid operation in the language, additional triples are created in an AST that the editor holds in its memory. This simple program in Listing 9.1 has 25 of these top-level triples organized into a hierarchy.

Underneath these triples are further related triples that describe the features of that particular operation (and its allowed features). Even for such a simple program, these would run many pages in a printed book (some elements of the description are potentially recursive, so the printout could be very long). However, the Inventory does not need all this information—it needs only what is relevant to the current problem. Thus, the tree can be pruned to provide the important information. Figure 9.3 shows a simplified view of Listing 9.1 in its tree form.

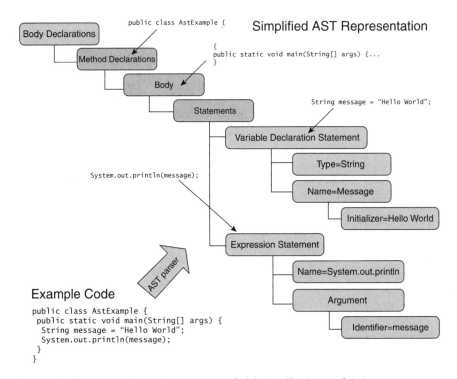

Figure 9.3 The code can be translated into a tree of triples just like the rest of the Inventory.

By definition, this hierarchical breakdown of the code must encompass all the possible variations within the language, so encoding more complex programs just involves more of the same.

The gulf between Views (whether expressed as spreadsheets, XML, UML, or now code itself) and the Inventory triples should not seem quite so wide as it perhaps did. With these Views transformed into perhaps millions of simple semantic triples, the key question now is, how are these put together in the Inventory?

Inventory

The Structure of the Inventory

As discussed previously, the core structure of the Inventory is very simple: It consists almost entirely of triples. Before we delve into the detail of the Inventory, it is important to understand the complexity that triples can support. The next section explains how triples work in more detail.

Triples

Triples are really simple English sentences in the form subject/verb/object. You can use these triples to relate items in everyday life.

Consider a simple example of a dinner party with four people; let's see how we can describe their social infrastructure using only triples. To keep this example brief, we will state only one triple, even though the inverse of the triple could also be stated. For example, "John is married to Janet" also implies (or could be assumed, given the nature of the marriage relationship and whether formal logic were applied) the inverse: "Janet is married to John." Figure 9.4 shows how this triple is shown in diagram form.

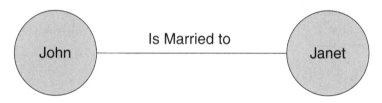

Figure 9.4 A simple Janet and John marriage triple

Note that in Figure 9.4, the triple is represented as two circles, or atoms, and a linking line. In formal diagrams, these straight lines are usually shown as arcs, but for the purposes of this description, straight lines suffice. Each of these lines has the description of the relationship (or verb) identified as text alongside it. Note here that if Janet and John had multiple triples linking them, then, for the purposes of simplifying these diagrams, the multiple triples would be represented as additional lines of descriptive text on the same line, not as additional lines. (Multiple lines or arcs is the standard convention but would make these diagrams unnecessarily complex.) However, you should still read the relationships as separate triples, not as one pair of atoms with multiple descriptions.

The dinner party consists of two couples, John and Janet (John is married to Janet), and Bob and Marilyn (Bob is married to Marilyn). The couples know each other because John used to be married to Marilyn. (John is divorced from Marilyn.) This is a simple model of the situation and would be a good first attempt at capturing the situation. However, as noted previously, Brownfield is an iterative process of information gathering.

As more information is uncovered, it is revealed that John and Marilyn had two children at the time of the divorce, David and Katie. They have remained good friends for the sake of their children. (John has child Katie; John has child David; Marilyn has child Katie; Marilyn has child David.)

Since John and Janet have gotten married, they have started their own family and now have a baby girl, Keira (John has child Keira; Janet has child Keira). David and Katie both live with their father (David resides with John; Katie resides with John). (We can also add that David resides with Janet; Katie resides with Janet.) Keeping up? More information has been added into the Inventory to further complete the picture.

As information about Bob and Marilyn is captured, it is discovered that Bob was also married previously, to someone outside the immediate group called Victoria. They had one child together, a boy called Tom (Bob has child Tom; Victoria has child Tom). It was a rather sad story: Victoria was killed in an automobile accident (Victoria has state deceased). Marilyn helped Bob get over the trauma, and now Tom lives with Bob and Marilyn (Tom resides with Marilyn; Tom resides with Bob). Figure 9.5 shows this information expressed in diagram form.

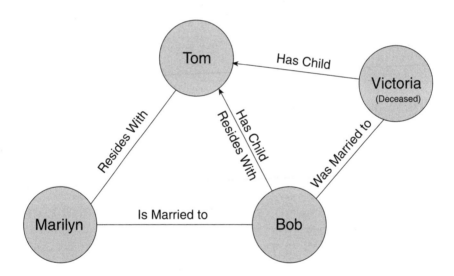

Figure 9.5   Bob and Marilyn's family triples

Further triples could be added to capture information such as age, sex, and address for each of our members to complete the picture. However, you can see the power of these simple triples: They have captured in a precise, unambiguous manner a complex social infrastructure that is difficult to explain in simple English.

However, care should be taken, in case some obvious information is missed. In the previous example, the Inventory does not contain information on whom

Keira resides with. Keira is John and Janet's new baby girl, so she resides with John and Janet (Keira resides with John; Keira resides with Janet).

This was implied but never stated explicitly. Care should be taken with triples to ensure that the implied information is also captured. For example, it is known that Keira resides with both John and Janet, but so do David and Katie. Therefore, it can be inferred that David and Katie reside with each other and also reside with Keira. This was never entered in the Inventory, although it can be inferred from the information already given. Figure 9.6 shows how this complex family information can be expressed as a diagram.

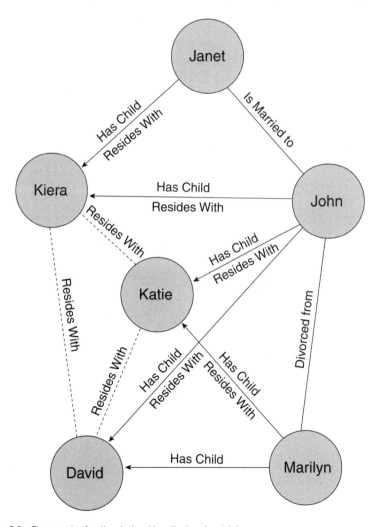

Figure 9.6   The complex family relationships displayed as triples

In Figure 9.6, the inferred links are shown as dotted lines. Some information already given has been left off this diagram because it is building into a complex diagram for two dimensions.

In a similar way, because David and Katie have the same parents, they can be seen as siblings. They could be brother and sister, but their sex has not yet been captured. This is the power of storing the data in the Inventory: The information that already has been imported can be used to infer other data. Perhaps this is obvious—why would a complex Inventory be required to determine something so obvious? The example given was indeed obvious because the information that was inferred was separated by only one degree of separation: Both children were linked by their parents. As the degree of separation increases, however, these relationships become less obvious, but links can be determined in the same manner from the Inventory.

In summary, the Inventory not only contains the captured information; it can also be used to infer further information and identify gaps in the information already supplied.

What if someone attempts to enter data that was incorrect? Let's say Bob is married to Janet. Figure 9.7 shows this incorrect information together with some of the already known information.

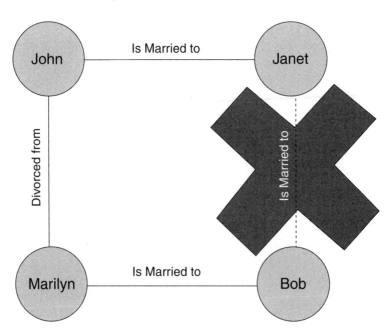

Figure 9.7 Inconsistent data becomes evident when looking at the triple relationships.

This cannot be true, for two reasons: Bob is already married to Marilyn, and Janet is already married to John. Therefore, the information in the Inventory shows an inconsistency in the data. For this reason, the importer will not allow this information to be entered. If for some reason it is now true (for example, Bob and Marilyn, and Janet and John got divorced), those relationships would have to be corrected before the previously rejected fact of Bob and Janet being married could be entered into the Inventory.

Another error situation might not be so obvious: Suppose that John's father is entered into the Inventory—he is called Peter (Peter has child John). This would be perfectly acceptable within the Inventory. But now attempting to enter that David is Peter's father (David has child Peter) highlights an error (see Figure 9.8).

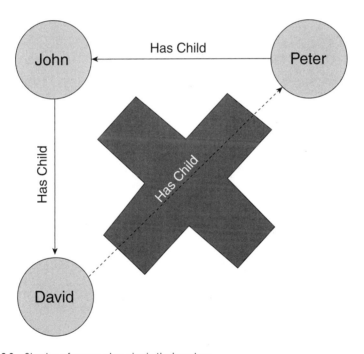

Figure 9.8   Circular references also arise in the Inventory.

This cannot be true. Peter is John's father, John is David's father, and David is Peter's father. Without trying to turn this into a sort of science fiction, time-travel paradox, the situation is impossible. This *circular reference* makes it invalid within the Inventory. The information will not be permitted in the Inventory because it will make the information inconsistent.

Triples not only allow the capture of this information in an unambiguous and consistent manner; they also enable you to check the data for consistency.

Triples are extremely useful for containing and supporting all the knowledge that is found about the project, but the Inventory itself needs a structure beyond that of the simple triples. Any system of this type needs to introduce some additional structure to make it maintainable and usable.

IBM has built and patented the structure for such an Inventory, as reproduced in Figure 9.9.

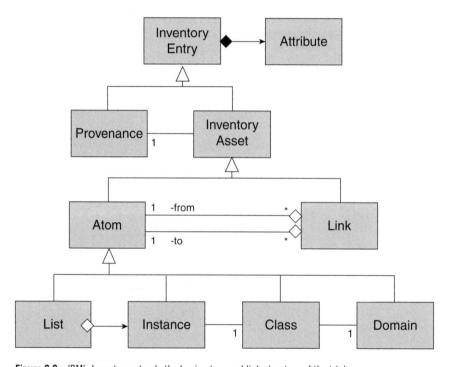

Figure 9.9   IBM's Inventory extends the basic atom and link structure of the triples.

The diagram is rather technical because it is expressed in UML, but the following key points are important:

- Inventory assets can be either atoms (also known as nodes) or links (also known as properties, arcs, or predicates).
- A link is a directional relationship between two atoms (from and to).
- Each asset in the Inventory (whether an atom or a link) must have a provenance to describe where it came from and when.

- Different kinds of atoms can correspond to things, lists of things, types of things (classes), and areas of the Inventory (domains).

- Every instance atom that represents a concrete item (a thing) must belong to a class atom that describes its contents and behavior.

- Each type of thing in the Inventory (the class atoms) must be ascribed to a domain (Business, Logical, Physical) that describes its position in the hierarchy of models and information.

- Although not shown, each Inventory entry has a mandatory "from" and "to" set of time-based attributes that describe the valid period(s) for that entry. This gives the Inventory a necessary time dimension, to allow for evolution over time.

These simple rules give an overall shape to the Inventory, making it easier to understand and deploy on projects. This is actually the meta-meta-model of an Inventory—it describes the high-level language of atoms and links. As you have already seen, almost any concept can be described using this approach—this structure is still very simple and extensible. This diagram does not define or impose a particular structure or specific language on the Inventory—individual projects can design and determine those (as with the metamodel in Figure 4.8 in Chapter 4, "The Trunk Road to the Brain").

Over time, Inventory languages (ontologies) likely will arise for different purposes. A single ontology for IT might be achievable one day, but for many of the reasons covered earlier when discussing the development of a grand universal tool, a powerful and all-embracing formal language will not likely be created. For an example of a language that we have used with the Inventory, see the Business Architecture metamodel in Figure 4.8 in Chapter 4.

The next short section outlines some of the key technologies used in the Inventory and is necessarily technical in nature. Readers who don't like acronyms and XML might want to jump to Step 2, where we move on to talk about how the Inventory is put together.

Owls and Elephants

The content of IBM's Inventory is expressed via the Web Ontology Language (OWL) and the Resource Description Framework (RDF). Both come from a family of frameworks created by the World Wide Web Consortium (W3C) to enable the semantic Web. RDF enables resources and relationships between resources to be described in XML form. RDF Schema extends this by incorporating the capability to express properties, classes, and hierarchies. OWL takes this yet further and provides a mechanism of describing relationships between these classes. The RDF metadata model enshrines the principle of the triple (subject, verb [or predicate], object), as you might expect.

The Inventory data can be stored in standard relational database management systems such as DB2®, SQL Server, or Oracle in specially configured triple stores.

When extracted, the Inventory data can be turned into text (a serialized form) for import or export to other Inventories. One such form is N-Triples (similar to the table view of the subject, verb, object list shown earlier in Table 9.2); another is the widely used RDF/XML. Listing 9.2 gives the simple UML example shown earlier in Figure 9.2 translated into RDF/XML. You don't need to understand this example to understand the rest of this chapter; it merely illustrates what an Inventory looks like in text form. (Such a form is not intended to be easily human readable.)

Listing 9.2 Translation of Figure 9.2 into RDF/XML

```
<?xml version="1.0"?>
<rdf:RDF
  xmlns="http://www.elephanteaters.org/example#"
  xmlns:rdf="http://www.w3.org/1999/02/22-rdf-syntax-ns#"
  xmlns:xsd="http://www.w3.org/2001/XMLSchema#"
  xmlns:rdfs="http://www.w3.org/2000/01/rdf-schema#"
  xmlns:owl="http://www.w3.org/2002/07/owl#"
  xml:base="http://www.elephanteaters.org/example" >
  <rdf:Description rdf:about="#isOfferedBy">
  <rdf:type rdf:resource="http://www.w3.org/1999/02/
➥22-rdf-syntax-ns#Property"/>
  <rdfs:range rdf:resource="#System"/>
  <rdfs:domain rdf:resource="#Interface"/>
  </rdf:Description>
  <rdf:Description rdf:about="#ViewEditor">
  <rdf:type rdf:resource="#System"/>
  <uses rdf:resource="#I_InventoryManagement"/>
  </rdf:Description>
  <rdf:Description rdf:about="#System">
  <rdf:type rdf:resource="http://www.w3.org/2002/07/owl#Class"/>
  </rdf:Description>
  <rdf:Description rdf:about="#Interface">
  <rdf:type rdf:resource="http://www.w3.org/2002/07/owl#Class"/>
  </rdf:Description>
```

```
<rdf:Description rdf:about="#offers">
<rdfs:domain rdf:resource="#System"/>
<rdf:type rdf:resource="http://www.w3.org/1999/02/
➡22-rdf-syntax-ns#Property"/>
<rdfs:range rdf:resource="#Interface"/>
</rdf:Description>
<rdf:Description rdf:about="#uses">
<rdfs:range rdf:resource="#Interface"/>
<rdf:type rdf:resource="http://www.w3.org/1999/02/
➡22-rdf-syntax-ns#Property"/>
<rdfs:domain rdf:resource="#System"/>
</rdf:Description>
<rdf:Description rdf:about="#System_A">
<rdf:type rdf:resource="http://www.w3.org/2002/07/owl#Thing"/>
</rdf:Description>
<rdf:Description rdf:about="#I_InventoryManagement">
<rdf:type rdf:resource="#Interface"/>
<isOfferedBy rdf:resource="#Inventory"/>
<isUsedBy rdf:resource=" "#ViewEditor"/>
</rdf:Description>
<rdf:Description rdf:about="#Inventory">
<offers rdf:resource="#I_InventoryManagement"/>
<rdf:type rdf:resource="#System"/>
</rdf:Description>
<rdf:Description rdf:about="#System_">
<rdf:type rdf:resource="http://www.w3.org/2002/07/owl#Thing"/>
<rdf:Description rdf:about="#isUsedBy">
<rdf:type rdf:resource="http://www.w3.org/1999/02/22-rdf-syntax-
ns#Property"/>
<rdfs:domain rdf:resource="#Interface"/>
<rdfs:range rdf:resource="#System"/>
</rdf:Description>
</rdf:RDF>
```

The area highlighted in bold is an example triple that says the Inventory
(which is a System) offers the Inventory Management interface.

An alternative way of representing this information is as an RDF graph
(see Figure 9.10). Unfortunately, you might not find this representation particularly helpful.

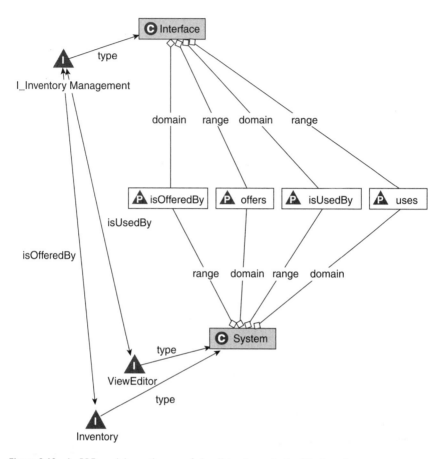

Figure 9.10   An RDF graph is another way of visualizing the contents of the Inventory.

The RDF (even in graph form) might seem quite unwieldy compared to the simple diagram or tables shown earlier in this book. Why would such a verbose mechanism be used to express the Inventory? The key reason is that the Inventory needs to be used as the base information for multiple transformations. The W3C frameworks are based on XML, so there are readily available technologies, tools, and skills for transforming the Inventory data into what we want (such as XSLT). Ultimately, the definition of the Inventory could be proprietary, but it would be far more useful if information could easily be exchanged between Inventories (especially during company merger talks). As Inventories become common, it would not be in the interests of our clients or the IT industry if the Inventories were proprietary or closed. The W3C technologies enable us to export and reimport Inventory data easily and exchange data among multiple industry-standard tools.

The emergence of the semantic Web (in which the natural language information on the Web is enhanced by including formal metadata that enables software agents to use and automatically generate it) means that future IT and Web services will want to be augmented with the kind of data we stored in the triples. The W3C frameworks should enable an Inventory user to achieve a leadership position in this new area. Indeed, RDF, RDFS, and OWL make the Inventory a key mechanism for sharing data and services, as well as consolidating and modernizing it. This is very different from the proprietary mentality of the CASE tools of the 1990s and will be central to the success and business cases for implementing Brownfield tooling.

Step 2: Merge Views

For nontechnical readers who read the last bit, thanks for staying with us! That page of RDF/XML extract is the only codelike bit in the book (although we do refer to it once more).

To understand how the different Views can be merged to form a single Inventory, it is worth taking a closer look at the component model example discussed earlier.

In this example, two separate source programs (View A and View B) show how two separate Views can be combined to create a single Inventory. The example is deliberately simplistic but gives a good idea of how the Inventory is created from separate but related sources of information.

View A is the Inventory program itself. First, the parsing process has turned the program into an AST. Looking for the right patterns in that source program makes it relatively straightforward to identify that the program offers an Inventory Management interface.

The program that forms View B, the View Editor, is treated similarly. The AST created from that program contains another interesting pattern. The View Editor program now offers only one interface that returns the View; it also calls two other programs. One of these interface calls is used to publish the content of the View; the other is used to send the View to the Inventory.

Figure 9.11 shows the information that has been extracted from analyzing each of these independent source code files expressed as two separate Views.

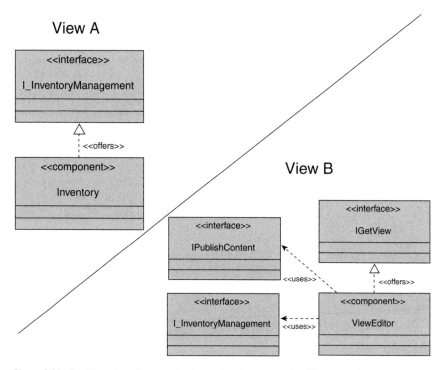

Figure 9.11   Two Views have been created by parsing the source code of two separate programs.

When the parsed program is imported into the Inventory, View A translates into two atoms and two links. (The single arrow is translated into two offers and isOfferedBy links that enable the relationship to be navigated easily in both directions.)

On the subsequent import of View B, the import program registers a shared atom between Views A and B. This shared atom is I_InventoryManagement. Upon recognizing this, the Inventory merging process discards the duplicate atom from View B and links the new information from View B to the entry from View A. The View B atom represents a "called" interface, not the actual interface itself, so the View A atom takes precedence.

The end result is a single merged Inventory expressed in RDF as represented in Figure 9.12.[1]

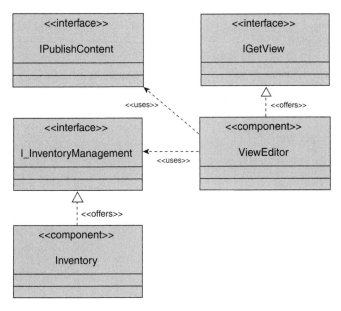

Figure 9.12 The Inventory attempts to merge the two Views, but this causes a problem—the Inventory is no longer valid.

Step 2a: Identify Missing or Incorrect Information

During this merging process, the combination of Views could result in a problem. These problems are often identified by enforcing the cardinality of allowed relationships within the Inventory.

When constructing the Inventory, a formal ontology (or language) is created for the Inventory to use. This ontology describes all the valid relationships allowed between different types of atoms and even specifies whether the relationship is optional or mandatory. If it is mandatory, the ontology specifies how many of these kinds of relationships should exist.

In the previous example, the formal relationships of "uses" and "offers," plus their opposites, isUsedBy and isOfferedBy, were defined to be in place between components and interfaces.

The Inventory created in Figure 9.12 is perfectly consistent with this and would not raise any errors upon merging. But what happens if it is mandated that all interfaces must be offered by at least one component—that is, for the model to be complete, something must actually implement what the interface is promising to do?

If this is mandated, the resulting merged Inventory in Figure 9.12 has information of an IPublishContent interface, but this interface has no implementing component—nothing "offers" the interface.

This could be a sign of incomplete data, or it might actually mark the edge of knowledge of the Inventory. However, if there *must* be at least one isOfferedBy relationship for every interface atom in the Inventory, then the Inventory is invalid. The missing relationship will be highlighted so that it can be corrected by including another View (perhaps the source code of the Publishing program) or correcting a View to include or delete the missing information.

Clearly, the same logic applies not just for the cardinality of relationships (whether a relationship is optional or mandatory, and how many are allowed between different types of atoms), but also for the relationships themselves.

Sharp-eyed (or die-hard technical) readers might have noticed Listing 9.3 in the XML/RDF file reproduced earlier:

Listing 9.3 Constraints on Relationships

```
<rdf:Description rdf:about="#isUsedBy">
<rdf:type rdf:resource="http://www.w3.org/1999/02/
➥22-rdf-syntax-ns#Property"/>
<rdfs:domain rdf:resource="#Interface"/>
<rdfs:range rdf:resource="#System"/>
</rdf:Description>
```

This states that isUsedby can be a relationship only from an interface (its domain) to a System (its range of targets).

If during processing, a View states that a component isUsedBy an interface, clearly the View is in error and must be amended.

Dimensions in Time

The Inventory is essentially a multidimensional space with a time dimension. Information can be extracted from it via slices through that space and time. Visualizing it as a whole is not easy.

This is not surprising. By definition, the Inventory contains multiple Views, and the amount of information it contains would be beyond what a single person could understand. Nevertheless, it is possible to take many different—but always consistent—slices through the Inventory after it is built. These can be chosen as View-size slices that one person can comprehend.

The best slice to take varies, depending on the audience. The slice chosen might provide a View on the Inventory that differs from the other Views that were fed in. This ability to see consistent data in varying ways and at different levels of abstraction is the core strength of the VITA architecture.

Figure 9.13 shows an Inventory with Views being imported from a variety of sources. There are three sources of information used to feed in site survey information. (Luckily, in this case, there were formal design materials, so no code parsing is necessary.) The following information is shown being fed into the Inventory:

- The infrastructure definition of the operational model (the infrastructure of the environment) is contained in an Eclipse-based tool called Architects' Workbench.[2] To import this data into the Inventory, an Eclipse-based triple converter was used to migrate from the Eclipse Modeling Framework (EMF) to triples. The operational model also contains information about how the system infrastructure supports the realized components in the component model. (This information is represented in Figure 9.13 by the black circles in the Inventory.)

- The business processes, business entities, and business process definitions are imported from WebSphere® Business Modeler. The naming convention used clearly indicates which use cases are being executed at which points in the business process. The export from this tool is in Business Process Execution Language (BPEL) and XML forms. Specially written Transforms convert this XML-based data into triples. (This information is represented in the diagram by the gray circles in the Inventory.)

- Finally, the logical external design of the system in the component model (which comprises both component specifications and component realizations) is fed in from IBM Rational Software Architect (RSA). The component model also contains the full definition of the systems context so that all use case interactions—whether with users or systems (these would be identified as the primary and secondary actors in the Use Cases)—can be traced via sequence diagrams to operations on component interfaces. (This information is represented in the diagram by the white circles in the Inventory.)

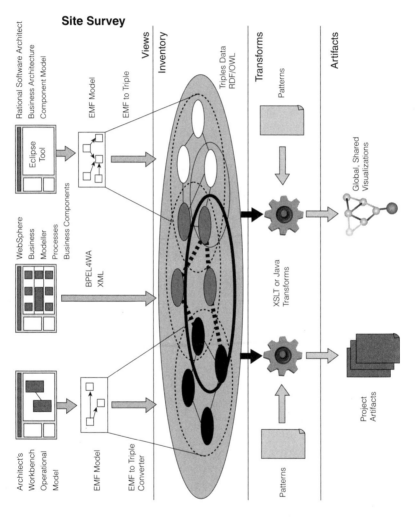

Figure 9.13 Multiple Views are combined in the Inventory so that the resulting data extracts can be used for all kinds of new purposes.

As this information is fed in, the links among the operational model, component model, use cases, sequence diagrams, and business process flows are established in the Inventory. In this case, it is lucky that the Inventory was always the target for this information; naming standards have been created and agreed upon in the tools, so the links between these sources of information can be automatically created (shown by the thick dotted lines between the circles).

Even if the information predates the intention to create an Inventory, the kind of traceability between documentation that the Inventory encourages is precisely the kind of information that should be looked for during static tests in the design process. Indeed, many people tacitly and repeatedly create such information in their heads during the design process (which, of course, takes time and introduces errors), so creating mappings or revising documentation in line with standards might be a good investment in its own right.

The Sum Is Greater Than the Parts

After the Inventory has been created by merging these sources, it is possible to extract information that was not present in the discrete Views. This is shown by the thick black circle within the Inventory. The information combined from all three sources can be extracted and used for a variety of purposes. This might include generating a performance model, checking the completeness of the operational and component models, generating deployment descriptors for Web services, and so on. The business architecture visualization perspective described in Chapter 4 can be produced from just such an extract from the Inventory. The list goes on and on.

The key aspect to grasp, however, is that all those outputs (including the visualization) can be generated from the Inventory information combined with patterns and templates. These outputs would also be absolutely consistent with the Inventory.

As any of the source Views change, the generated components are also quickly regenerated. Any new inconsistencies created by the updates are highlighted by the merging process of the Inventory. Clearly, this is a huge productivity and quality benefit for any large project because it massively reduces the communication overhead between teams. Different perspectives of this Inventory can be generated to help describe the problem to different audiences, to manage the complexity and set expectations. Importantly, these Views all look at the same problem and iron out inconsistencies when the Inventory is created. Everything can then be generated from the same consistent set of data. Using traditional means, on the other hand, would have required rewriting the information manually, often using multiple incomplete or inconsistent sources; this would introduce a source of error and maintenance overhead.

In addition, each entry in the Inventory has its own provenance (who created it, when it was created, what tool the information came from, and so on). As a result, the input of each atom or link can be traced back to the user and even the View that entered it into the Inventory. Because these Views include formal representations of the requirements for the solution, traceability from requirement through to generated Artifact is ensured.

Precision Architectures

Before we leave our description of the Inventory, we should consider one other important property: inference. We have shown that the Elephant Eater can suck in data from a wide variety of sources and interrelate it. If inconsistencies are spotted, they are highlighted at the time of import. A fair complaint about the Inventory, therefore, is that it contains a lot of interrelated stuff. How on earth can you see the forest for the trees? Well, some sources of data (for example, the formal architecture or design descriptions) might already be at a reasonable level of abstraction to be understood, but that is not likely true of undocumented source code.

Fortunately, the Inventory makes it possible to formally re-create architectural-level material from source code. Unlike the architecture pictures that are drawn early in a project and turn out to be incomplete, inaccurate, or simply massive oversimplifications of the truth, these pictures are precise and complete. (Even if they are high level, they can be precise and correct.) If the Views contain clearly structured data, the process of creating some architectural-level information is relatively trivial. Consider a simple example in Figure 9.14 in which the following relationships can be read:

- The View Editor has a View Publisher component.
- The View Publisher component uses the Inventory Management interface.
- The Inventory Management interface is offered by the Import Handler component.
- The Import Handler component is part of the Inventory system.

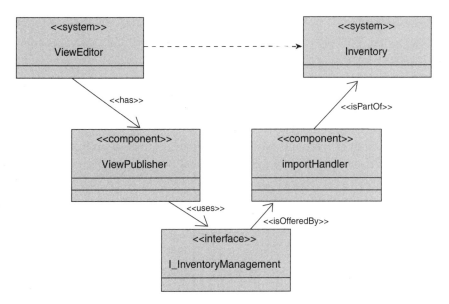

Figure 9.14   From the complex underlying relationships, it can be inferred that the View Editor uses the Inventory.

Clearly, it would be just as useful and accurate, but much shorter and clearer, to say "The View Editor uses the Inventory," which is inferred via the dotted arrow at the top. Just as the Inventory can identify the wrong or missing relationships (see Step 2a earlier), it can infer such implied links at varying levels of depths or abstraction—it simply needs to be told which chains of relationships to look for. In this case, it would be a chain that could be written in English as follows:

A system has a component, which uses an interface, which is offered by a component, which is part of a system.

When it finds such a chain in the Inventory, the system can infer a new relationship, which is "system uses system." This allows the complexity of the Inventory to be accurately summarized into higher-level drawings or architectures. Automatically providing such easy-to-absorb but precise information is a key strength of the Brownfield approach. These abstract links are different from those created from Views because their provenance is within the Inventory itself. As the Inventory is modified, these inferred links must be revalidated because the links that brought them into existence could have disappeared. This offers the further benefit that inferred links do not become a separate View to be maintained; the Inventory creates them after each merge.

Not all such Brownfield sites are sufficiently well documented to follow this approach. In these cases, the process of formal abstraction is a path of inference and builds up a picture layer by layer.

Today's formal methods start trying to break down a problem by first ignoring what happens within the system and just understanding the external interactions that need to take place with the exterior of the system. You can think of the system as a black box. Once you understand the external interactions, you can look at what is happening inside the system; it is as if the light has been turned on for that system—it is essentially a white box. This white box can then be broken down into further components. These components themselves are seen as black boxes until the interactions are defined. Then their lights are turned on and their internals can be examined.

Essentially, today's formal methods create a system by incrementally creating black-box descriptions of the solution required, working out the necessary internals to the next level of detail (white box) and then using those elements to frame a black-box description of what is required. The cycle then repeats. Figure 9.15 shows this black box, white box iteration (termed a "zebra" approach).

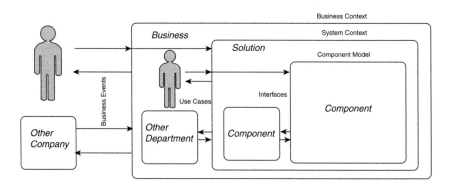

Figure 9.15   The black box, white box iteration enables the boundaries of various levels of the problem or solution to be described without specifying an implementation.

A typical large project follows this type of procedure, as shown graphically in Figure 9.15:

1. Identify the boundary of the business in a business context, and define all the business events that flow over that boundary (Black Box 1).

2. Using the business context as the scope and the business events as the starting point for processes, document the flow of work around the organization (White Box 1).

3. When the business processes are being created, identify the points at which the business process will need to access a system. Determine whether that access is within or outside the scope of the solution under design. Use these points to create the systems context and to identify the use cases that flow over the systems context (Black Box 2).

4. Determine from walking through and completing the use cases what capabilities the solution will need. Define high-level components that have distinct responsibilities and are relatively independent of each other in the component model (White Box 2).

5. For each of those components, describe a set of operations on an interface that tell what it must do. Describe the information it needs to do those operations and what the outcome of those operations is (Black Box 3).

6. For each of the components, identify how each of them will work in the application design (White Box 3).

This is a powerful approach because the successive black boxes tell the next layer down what they must do, without imposing a particular structure or solution.

Brownfield often appears to reverse Greenfield processes, so you won't be too surprised to learn that precise architectures are abstracted from code by reversing these last three steps and putting the layers back on the onion where they have been lost.

For example, this Brownfield approach has been used to successfully impose a component model onto a solution that had grown (relatively organically) a formal data model and had no such structure. This encouraged some restructuring of the solution. As a result, the number of developers who could work on the solution in parallel increased.

The reversal of this process is as follows:

1. Identify the formal interfaces in the source code via the AST and pattern identification approach.

2. Analyze the calling and offering relationships in the source code to identify which areas are linked to each other.

3. Some components (such as a database) can be called from many points in the system, and these can easily be identified as calls between layers in the architecture.

4. After identifying the layers, you can identify the components within those layers. Certain elements within a layer call each other a lot; others hardly talk at all. Generating a UML diagram from the Inventory and loading it into a tool can help with this process because it requires some judgment as well as simple analysis. This resulting output is a new View that maps the programs into components.

5. The Inventory can now work out interface-level structures by inferring direct "uses" and "offers" relationships between the components that have been identified by inferring them from the interfaces within the source code (as shown in our simple example earlier in Figure 9.14).

These new components, with formally identified interfaces and relationships, can be used to refactor the existing system or, alternatively, to generate modern facades (such as Web services), advertising a structure that was always there but previously hidden, accidental, emergent, or forgotten. Before you get too excited, however, we should tell you that Brownfield is more akin to archaeology than magic. If there genuinely was no structure to begin with, only chaos, there would be little or no structure to uncover.

Transforms

As you saw in Chapter 3, VITA optionally uses Transforms to create links between related concepts in the Inventory. Sometimes it is enough to simply indicate that two concepts are related in an informal way via a simple relationship. At other times, it might be advantageous to understand how to transform between them.

How Does the Single Version of the Truth Cope with a Million Shades of Gray?

Each transformation is really three separate stages: classification of the data structures to be transformed, the actual transformation of those structures, and the application of any constraints. So what is meant by *transformations*?

Consider a simple example: Suppose that two systems within our enterprise have a date of birth stored. The first of these stores them in the American format of MM/DD/YY, whereas another system stores it in a format of DD/MM/YY, a format commonly used in Europe. Both represent the same date, just stored in a different manner. In this case, the transformation would have a relatively simple job of moving the first two sets of numbers to complete the transformation. So, transformations can be very easy. This likely would be a normal transformation that could be chosen from the Inventory as it's a standard transformation. But suppose that it wasn't.

The transformation is potentially very simple. It has one input (MM/DD/YY) and one output (DD/MM/YY). So it would be relatively easy to describe a transformation within the tooling to say what it has to do. Transpose the characters before the first / and the characters before the second /. A programmer could now create such a routine to do such a conversion. Because it is a relatively simple routine with minimal inputs and outputs and a simple description, it would be simple to develop. To avoid any programmer confusion, you could also specify some examples or test data to use with the appropriate results. For example, 12/21/07 becomes 21/12/07.

Assume now that the routine was written but seemed to fail when used on real data. It seems that the routine worked fine on the data when two characters were used, but not when one character was used to represent a month or day in the month. For example, 1/23/07 returned 3/21/07. The problem was not specified completely, and the programmer misunderstood and used literal positions for moving the data. This is a common mistake that frequently happens in system development. The description of the problem is often incomplete, and mistakes are then detected during testing.

The description is changed to state this and also give another few examples of data to convert (1/23/07 becomes 23/1/07). Now when the new routine is created, the Inventory can automatically test the transformation and reject it if it fails the test cases.

This simple example shows how transformations can be defined in a nonprogrammatic manner. It also illustrates how data transformation can be broken down into very small, simple, self-contained Transforms and can potentially be built anywhere. This is great when you are using a global sourcing model and one of the most difficult problems is precisely defining the requirements of what you want. This should be relatively simple here, and the Inventory tooling itself will provide an automated means of testing the results when completed.

Let's extend the example slightly. Suppose that the format to convert from was the same, but the format to convert to was now DD/MM/YYYY. The day and month part of the transformation should be the same as described earlier; the difference here is that the year must now be converted from two to four digits.

If the year had to be converted from four to two digits, this would be extremely simple—the first two digits could just be dropped. However, in doing that operation, some of the original information is lost—the precise century that this date occurred. So, in reversing this operation and extending the year from two to four digits, we have to define some rules to make up this information.

If the same situation occurred in real life, it might be possible to make some assumptions and define this in rules to make up this missing data. For the sake of argument, assume that the original database contains only adults (over 18 years of age). You could use a 100-year window, 18 years behind the current year. Someone who had a year of 98 in the original data, would be assumed to be born in 1898 instead of 1998, because someone born in 1998 would not yet be an adult. This would work well in most cases for people up to the age of 118 years old. For the moment, that would seem a reasonable compromise. However, if the data was not all adults, that would make it correct for only people up to 100 years old. This might not be completely unreasonable, but you will be wrong a bit more often because there are more people of this age.

If the data was not even restricted to people who were currently alive, however, this solution would be totally unacceptable.

Although it might not be possible to determine the correct year with the birth date and the incomplete year specification, it might be possible to use some other information in the records to take a more educated approach to determining this year.

In looking through the available information, another field apparently was specified that contained a person's age when he or she started dealing with the organization and the year in which this occurred (in four digits). The correct year of birth can be precisely determined using these three items of information. Although this is a very simple transformation, it illustrates that transformations are reversible. The simple date change in the first two-digit year can be reversed simply because no information is lost in the original transformation. In the case of changing a four-digit year to two digits, information is lost and the transformation may be reversed only by applying rules or combining data from a number of resources to re-create that information. However, in both cases the reverse transformation was possible.

This solution will work on dates of birth, but the same solution cannot be used for death dates, for example (although the same data could be used in a slightly different manner). Thus, it is important for the original data to be classified correctly before the transformation is defined. The original data would be classified as a date of birth and not just as a date. In this way, the correct transformation could be chosen for the correct date.

But there are really three parts to a transformation. The last of these is the application of constraints. These constraints determine whether the data that has been transformed will be included in the output. For example, a constraint could be applied so that bank account details are sent only if the person is applying for a loan; otherwise, that person will be left out. Although this is a very simple example, it again illustrates the basics of transformations.

To summarize, first, all data is categorized, then the Transforms are defined between these categories and other categorized data, and, finally, in defining the data sharing required between systems, the categories and Transforms are combined with constraints to determine exactly what is shared.

Step 3: Create Transforms

This Transform capability is often used when the Inventory is being used as a source of information to generate interfaces, gateways, enterprise service buses, or other forms of integration between systems. The concepts in System A and System B are mapped, and a simple reusable Transform is identified in the Inventory that can migrate the data from one format to another.

These atomic Transforms can be expressed as XSLT or as small programs that are then called upon when the Inventory generates an Artifact that needs to transform between two representations of the data or concept.

Artifacts

Artifacts were described in Chapter 3 to cover all outputs that can be generated from the Inventory information. Typically, these outputs include documentation, configuration, executables, and test Artifacts.

Documentation Artifacts are used to describe those outputs that are generated to describe the system, and even include the visualization Artifacts described in Chapter 4. Such documentation is always consistent with your solution and up-to-date.

Configuration Artifacts are used to provide the definition, setup, or control of products or systems within your IT estate. These may be for structures such as databases.

Executable Artifacts cover all generated Artifacts that are run within a computer system to perform a business task. This includes program code, user interface screens, interface definitions, or rules for business rules engines.

Test Artifacts are used for the testing of the output of the executable or configuration Artifacts. These may take the form of test scripts and the generation of the data required to test the system thoroughly.

Step 4: Generate Artifacts

Extracts can be produced from the Inventory—the Inventory can provide subsets of itself (usually represented by a single point in time and a "slice" through the Inventory data) to generate Artifacts.

These Artifacts are the standard stuff of Model Driven Development and Architecture, so we do not cover them in detail in this book. However, the capability to represent the Inventory in RDF/XML is a considerable boon because XSLT can create templates from which Artifacts can be generated. XSLT also ensures a clean separation between patterns and templates and the data from the Inventory.

Paying Your Own Way

Clearly, performing the site survey, buying tooling, and feeding information into the Inventory is a significant investment. The Inventory delivers its own benefits and pays its own way via the following:

- Improved quality of Artifacts
- Improved reuse of Artifacts and patterns at all levels
- Improved conformance to patterns and architectures
- Automated generation and unit testing of Artifacts
- Earlier testing via visualization and early executable tests, for reduced cost of defect removal

Artifacts are not just simple perspectives or slices through the Inventory. The factory-based generator has been used to create all kinds of different Artifacts—for example, from data structures, interfaces Transforms, code, and even the documentation of the problem itself. Thus, the documentation always remains completely up-to-date and consistent. As described in ISO 9000, "You do what you document and you document what you do."

Steps 5.1: Test Artifacts and
5.1a: Identify Generation Faults

The generated code Artifacts are tested automatically against validation code generated for this purpose. These tests are created from the same problem definition (via a different generation route) so that the generated tests' coverage of the problem definition is known to be complete, and so that the data used in the tests (which is also generated) is consistent with what is expected. Negative testing (that is, testing values known to be outside the correct functioning of the component or interface) can also be performed.

This testing ensures that the solution does precisely what was expected—therefore, the problem has been correctly translated into a solution. Now, a system testing itself might seem poor practice, but these tests cover a large portion of what unit testing normally does in terms of industry best practices (that is, essentially, write a comprehensive test specification first and then write the code). Clearly, this automated testing cannot identify whether the description of the problem (the requirement) is wrong, although it can often identify that it is incomplete or inconsistent. Either way, this automation is a significant productivity benefit and removes defects early.

An additional benefit of Brownfield development is that because the exact composition of any generated solution is known (in terms of the data used to populate the pattern and the pattern[s] used), change impacts become manageable. Within the Brownfield approach, the impact of any change in requirement or design can determined by deriving all the affected components—and all the test cases needed to exercise the complete test coverage for a regression test.

Step 5.1b: Add and Update Information

As previously discussed, Brownfield is primarily an iterative approach for complex problems. As further requirements (normally, constraints) are discovered during testing, they can be added to the Views and the new version of the solution generated, with no degradation of the design or code.

A Portrait of an Elephant Eater

In this chapter, we have offered some insight into what is contained within the tooling required to support Brownfield. The tooling is based upon open industry standards of XML, RDF, and OWL, which also are used to support the semantic Web.

The Brownfield tool itself does not support the development process; other tools are necessary for that. Instead, it imports information from other tools and links it together. Various importers have been written to convert the Views exported from the tools into the triples format that the Inventory supports. This combines the information from diverse tools that are used for different parts of the solution (for example, the component model, operational model, and business process model).

Such formal documentation rarely exists on legacy systems, so code can even be parsed to reverse-engineer the documentation required. This is not a simple code conversion; it builds up the underlying patterns and structures within the legacy code by using AST.

All this information is converted into the simple triple structure used within the Inventory. To make the information more useful and easier to navigate, a simple meta-meta-model extends the triple model to provide more shape to the Inventory. Provenance is also added via this meta-meta-model so that, for each item in the inventory, its source version and time validity is always known.

Solutions also must produce their own ontology (language) in these triples, to provide further structure. In the future, these could become consolidated into standard ontologies perhaps grouped by industry, which will further simplify the process of Brownfield development.

When the information is contained within the Inventory, it is ensured to be consistent because it is validated upon entry. This large volume of information provides a baseline of the information provided and also allows further knowledge to be obtained. Either information can be inferred from the existing information or gaps in areas of knowledge can be identified.

Transformations are defined between data so that the Inventory can identify the transformations required in transferring data between different systems.

Finally, the most powerful part of the Inventory is that it can be used to generate a variety of Artifacts that document, test, or provide the physical solution. This means that documentation can be created at the appropriate level for different audiences so that the audience will find it easier to understand the information. Artifacts used in the solution will have their own test Artifacts generated automatically. Whatever Artifacts are produced, they are always up-to-date and consistent.

In building an Elephant Eater, a tool is created that can handle the complexity of modern systems. It does not assume or ignore information. Solution development becomes an engineering process; it is not determined by a throw of the dice. Indeed, Brownfield provides a mechanism for agile, iterative development in the most complex environments. The iterative refinement of a system can be from both an operational and a functional perspective, with the capability to receive timely feedback on requirements or design changes.

Implementing an Elephant Eater is a nontrivial task, but Brownfield pays for itself through the generation of Artifacts and the early discovery of requirement defects. Unlike the benefits of enterprise architectures and other formal innovations such as systems engineering, the benefits of Brownfield can be easily measured against conventional approaches. Fortuitously, the application of the Brownfield development approach need not be adopted across the board, but may be prioritized on the key areas where the initial benefits are greatest, thus offsetting much of the initial investment and inevitable initial productivity hit of a new process and technology. These key areas are those that involve high degrees of code duplication—the standard fare for MDA—combined with areas of poor knowledge, where standard MDA fears to tread. In the final chapter, we examine these areas and describe how Brownfield can be deployed on a project.

Endnotes

[1]   The technical reader will recognize the diagram in Figure 9.12 as UML instead of an RDF-based graph. We think the RDF graph is less readable, but the Inventory has been used to generate such UML diagrams from parsed source code.

[2]   The Architects' Workbench is an internal IBM tool based on the open Eclipse platform used to capture information and produce architectural Artifacts. Because it captures this information in a formal manner, this information can be imported into the Inventory relatively simply.

The following references apply to the chapter material in general.

Coplien, James O. and Neil B. Harrison. *Organizational Patterns of Agile Software Development*. Pearson Education, 2005.

Krebs, Jochen. *Patterns in Action*. www.ibm.com/developerworks/rational/library/may06/krebs/.

Partridge, Chris. *Business Objects—Re-engineering for Re-Use*. Butterworth-Heinemann, 2005.

10

Elephant Eater at Work

"The longest journey begins with a single step."
—*Confucius*

Chapter Contents

- Making the Move to Brownfield   204
- Taking the First Step   207
- A Better Way to Build Interfaces   207
- A Better Way to Build an Enterprise Service Bus   209
- The End of Middleware?   211
- Evolving a Deployable Enterprise Architecture   212

Making the Move to Brownfield

This book has explained the problems that face the industry today in successfully completing elephantine projects. The success rate of these projects is extremely poor. The methods and processes used in these very large projects were essentially designed for projects that are Greenfield in nature, and they have remained fundamentally unchanged over the last 30 years.

Unfortunately, very few opportunities exist for elephantine Greenfield developments. In addition, most enterprises have a vast infrastructure in which the developments must reside, with large amounts of data that must be migrated from the existing systems. Yet the industry persists with methods designed for Greenfield-type developments.

The Brownfield development approach suggested in this book is based on extending the latest best practices within the IT industry, together with the site survey currently used in the construction industry, combined with some further elements borrowed from architects who build real buildings. After reading this book, the benefits of using a Brownfield development approach on any complex project should be obvious—the problem is how and where to start....

Building Your Own Elephant Eater

The problem of where to start is complicated by the fact that the approach is still new and the skills required to deliver solutions in a Brownfield way differ from normal skills. The core technologies make extensive use of XML, XSLT, Eclipse, RSA, semantic engineering, RDF, and OWL. Although most developers are familiar with the first four of those, the remaining three skills are relatively rare (although the last two are not *essential* to the Brownfield approach).

At the time of writing, no good tools exist for natively maintaining combined business and IT architectures—this is why we've opted for models and metamodels in RSA with the dynamic aspects in WebSphere Business Modeler. This could change over time, but currently, "roll your own" is the main option. In addition, there's no commercially available Inventory (yet). Some of the architecture tools out there have a subset of the Inventory capability, but if you want to do everything described in this book, you'll have to build one yourself. Ideally, we recommend building on something that already exists—we don't believe in Greenfield tool creation either.

In addition to having to roll your own Elephant Eater, you must choose a language for your Inventory. Formal ontologies (languages) expressed in triples for everything from business modeling to architecture and system designs have already been created. Many of them are published on the Internet. But these languages overlap, underlap, and are tricky to combine. No clear or single winner for an Inventory language has emerged yet. Until a great deal of further standardization occurs in this space via W3C, OMG, and ISO, the exchange of Inventories will remain complex.

More important than the skills and tools gap is the cultural investment in the Greenfield approaches that will take a lot of time to overcome. The IT industry has turned away from embracing complexity for many years. The idea of "abstraction first and getting to the detail later," testing "V" models, and the pedestrian-crossing alternation of black box/white box are endemic and often regarded as best practice. Therefore, you'll find an inherent conservatism in the IT industry.

The techniques we have described in this book are sufficiently novel that IBM has filed for patents to protect our particular implementation of Brownfield and the techniques we use to visualize the Inventory for testing purposes. Brownfield is not a research technology (it was created and is still maintained by field personnel), but it is new and novel.

When projects are very large and the risks are high, innovation tends to be introduced a little at a time. Brownfield came about only because of a persistent team of committed technical individuals were able to convince executives, colleagues, and clients that they had something that was worth investing in and exploiting. The next generation of Elephant Eaters will benefit from this book, new tooling, and further innovations, but change is always difficult.

However, even with these provisos, this kind of thought process is at the forefront of business and IT thinking. It will be some time before we have a new industry-accepted norm for business reengineering and modeling. But we need one!

Empowering Business Change

Ultimately, the biggest challenge of implementing Brownfield is actually one of culture. You've probably noticed that all the Views used in Brownfield to generate a solution need to be formal. This is not simply a question of using standard Visio or PowerPoint notations when developing business process models or business organization charts; it involves ensuring that those charts are created in tools that can export (and preferably) import their data in a computer-readable format.

But even more than that is involved: The way in which diagrams are drawn must be standardized. The data that forms the intersection point between Views must be sufficiently formal and agreed upon by both parties within each View. This is neither necessarily hard nor difficult to achieve because both sides should understand the intersections well. However, this introduces rigor and collaboration into areas with relatively informal documentation, with previous handover processes that consisted of merely "chucking it over a wall." Brownfield imposes an approach that mandates precision and collaboration. That in itself is not a bad thing, as long as the community that creates the Views still readily understands them.

On one large customer-management project that needed a complex scripted question set with more than 1,000 questions, the format of the questions also dictated the format of the forms to be sent to the customers. The scripted questions were modeled in a tool, and this was used to generate the Artifacts to create the appropriate forms.

Business analysts expressed initial trepidation and frustration toward using the modeling tools to manage the scripting process because of the precision in which they had to capture the information. Although theoretically they had already been capturing the information in a similar-looking format, they had been using Office drawing tools to do so, and precision had not been enforced.

Over time, this frustration turned to satisfaction as they realized that the diagrams and spreadsheets they were creating (the Views) directly dictated the output of what was produced. No one could interfere with or misinterpret the material they were creating. These business analysts were managing to directly generate solutions to customers' problems by precisely documenting the requirements.

—K.J.

Indeed, in our direct experience, after the initial trepidation of dealing with something new, business analysts and users *love* the idea that what they define gets put into the solution *without change*. No one can dilute or misinterpret their ideas or concepts with Brownfield—they are essentially engineering the solution. Isn't that how it should be?

Taking the First Step

If this book has convinced you to use Brownfield as a means of developing complex projects for your enterprise, how do you take the first step? Tools and industry capabilities are still developing, so no off-the-shelf tools are currently available. Inevitably, some developing of tools will be required.

Recommending that someone abandon existing practices and wholeheartedly adopt the Brownfield approach seems a huge risk when the stakes are so high. Indeed, the technical and cultural challenges encountered with such a radical approach will almost certainly lead to failure.

As with any new method, a better way is to introduce the approaches in this book into some aspects of the development. Then, as the tooling develops, cultural problems slowly are resolved, and confidence in the tooling increases, you can extend the approach into more areas.

Taking this slow approach to Brownfield will still give the project some of the benefits of the complete approach, and it will minimize the risk from tooling and cultural issues.

If you're not eating the whole elephant, what parts of the elephant are worthy of first nibbling? A suggested first step is the interfacing aspects of the project. In any part of today's solutions, interfaces are increasingly a major part of the development—they are also a major source of problems in elephantine developments.

Few solutions today have no interfaces to other systems. In the elephantine projects that are being considered here, none have no interfaces. That might sound like a bold statement, but it is true: Virtually all projects of the scale being considered require many interfaces to other systems.

A Better Way to Build Interfaces

Brownfield and MDA offer many advantages when it comes to developing interfaces. Perhaps one of the main advantages of developing such an interface is best illustrated by an analogy.

Consider that you have been asked to write a single-page story on a word processor. After you have finished the story, imagine that the editor gives you some more information to include in your story. Let's assume that your editor has asked you to state that the hero has a motorbike and that the heroine is a nurse. You include this by making some changes to a few sentences. The editor now asks that the story include the fact that the scene is a beach. You change a few more sentences.

Each time, you can include the new information by making a few small changes to a couple of sentences. At some point, as more changes are added, the main flow of the story will be lost and it will have to be rewritten. When code is written in a conventional manner, it is similar to the writing of this story. The code will need to be changed slightly to accommodate changes in requirements. It will often not be quite as good as if it was designed with those requirements from the start. As more changes to requirements are made, the structure of the code deteriorates. As with the story, at some point it should be rewritten, or it will be difficult to maintain.

This is a particular concern with elephantine developments. Often with interfaces, the full requirements of interfacing with a heritage system are not fully known or documented and must be discovered.

An example of such an interface being developed with incomplete requirements occurred when working on a major government project. The system needed to interface to a heritage system that could not be physically changed.

To accomplish this, the interface effectively emulated people entering information via terminals. This technique is a form of "screen scraping" and is commonly used when interfacing with heritage systems. It allows an interface to be built without requiring any changes to the heritage system itself. In the case of this interface, the definitions of the field data formats for every screen were known.

Seventeen screens were required to complete the whole process. The interscreen requirements weren't known. For example, suppose that the first screen included a field for the number of children; screen two then included fields to enter your children's names. Of course, you then discover a requirement that these two fields should be consistent. In this case, if you specified one child, there should be only one name. This is a simple example, but as the number of screens built up, the dependencies—and, hence, requirements—of these interfaces build up.

In this specific example, the field formats of the data on the screens accounted for only 12 percent of the total interface requirement— the interscreen dependencies and hidden internal business logic accounted for the rest. If you consider the example of the story written earlier, what is the chance that you will modify it so much without having to rewrite it? In fact, you might not have to rewrite it just once—you might have to rewrite it several times.

—K.J.

_____

Naturally, when developing such an interface using Brownfield techniques, the reason for each test failure is investigated. The reason normally is a constraint (remember, in Brownfield, these are seen as requirements) that was not previously captured. This constraint can now be updated into a source View as a new requirement and imported into the Inventory. From the Inventory, the updated solution can then be generated. This new updated solution satisfies the new constraint and all the previous constraints that existed for that interface. As this is generated, it is new code. Therefore, it does not contain the contamination of its earlier development history.

VITA provides a means of accommodating the discovery of the "new" constraints or requirements found during the testing. In the example described earlier, in which only 12 percent of the requirements were known at the start of development, it was possible to perform two complete iterations per day of the solution generation, complete testing, and incorporate the new constraints discovered in the testing. These iterations were all completed in a change-controlled and -managed process. Each iteration of the solution was an improvement on the previous one. It would be exceptionally difficult to accomplish this using a conventional Greenfield technique.

A Better Way to Build an Enterprise Service Bus

Elephantine solutions require linking the existing heritage application to new applications. Software known as middleware is used to link these applications. The introduction of Service Oriented Architectures (SOAs) that allow your applications to talk to each other via services has led to the development of new types of middleware. The Enterprise Service Bus (ESB) was created as this new form of middleware to control and manage these services.

ESBs provide a means of communicating between systems in the form of services. Each "service" on the ESB effectively translates the data from the source system to a common form used within the ESB. The ESB then converts this common form to the form required to every system.

This technique allows each service to be built separately. New systems can then use that service by simply creating a transformation (or translation) between the common form and its own specific form. In some ways, this is much like the generic Brownfield approach that allows everyone in the solution to speak in their own language. The ESB is used as the "translator" between these different systems.

The ESB is seen as the current nirvana in the field of system integration because each system effectively talks in its own language. Each individual system does not have to worry about the precise language required for the other side of the interface. Translation within the ESB handles the complexity. However, the Brownfield Inventory contains all the semantics and syntax of the source system, the common form within the ESB and the target system. That information is used to generate each of the required transformations to be built into the ESB. In this way, Brownfield now supports an ESB that will have its transformation configuration generated automatically and, more important, consistently.

Via the VITA principle described in Chapter 3, "Big-Mouthed Superhero Required," Brownfield allows each stage of the ESB process to be defined and captured in the Inventory. In Figure 10.1, this is the Systems A and B format together with the common form. To convert among these three formats, two Transforms within the ESB must be defined; Figure 10.1 also shows these.

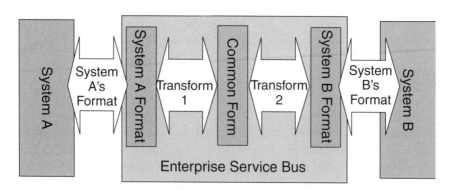

Figure 10.1 The formats and transformations required for an ESB service

After the definitions of the data interface between the two systems and the common format are defined within the Inventory, then the relationships, or transformations, between these forms can be defined and captured in the Inventory. The configurations required by the ESB to perform this service can then be generated from the Inventory.

Using a common form allows different systems to use the same service by just defining the relationships between its form and the standard form. This allows the enterprise to have little dependency on particular systems. If a system is changed within the enterprise, only the relationships to the common form need to be redefined; all other systems will remain untouched.

Although this is perhaps useful, it has automated only a couple stages in the process that were previously performed manually. It marks some progress but is hardly revolutionary. The process still doesn't seem to be taking full advantage of the fact that the Inventory holds the complete story.

An ESB performs more than just a translation service. It enables the enterprise to build up business processes by combining and linking these services. The term used to describe this is *choreography,* an apt name because the business processes can be thought of as a dance, with the services as the dance steps. Just as you choreograph a dance in terms of dance steps, you can choreograph your business processes in terms of services. The ESB contains all the information required to accomplish this.

However, the Inventory contains all the information about these business processes and the IT services available. The information required to produce the choreography is all sitting inside the Inventory. If the Inventory contains the information, that information can be used to generate the Artifacts that the ESB requires to control the choreography.

Brownfield has now used the Inventory to generate the entire configuration that the ESB requires. The configuration has all been generated from a single source of truth. As such, the configuration produced is entirely consistent. Brownfield now has managed to produce an easier way to keep control of the ESB. Brownfield allows the inputs for all the translations to be generated, along with any configurations required for the choreography. As such, the integration of the systems can be generated from a single source. This offers considerably more than just the generation of the translation aspects of the interface.

The End of Middleware?

Does Brownfield have more to offer to ESBs? The ESB enables you to keep control of your business processes within the ESB. Brownfield gives you control at a level above the ESB. This means that the ESB is effectively reduced to a collection of patterns and techniques to provide the integration required. The ESB controls all operations that pass through it in a generic way. If the

Inventory is now used to generate the configuration, it could also be used to generate the complete solution required to replace an ESB.

This would seem of little use because it is just replacing something that a business could purchase, with no real gain. This goes against one of the Brownfield beliefs to buy rather than create. However, ESBs are designed to pass messages in a very generic manner, as a simple way to maintain control of the business processes within the enterprise. Now Brownfield provides the area of control and can generate the solution in an optimal manner. Unnecessary translations can be removed, and business processes can be optimized. For example, translations could be performed directly instead of in stages via the common form. This is similar to translating directly between English and German rather than accomplishing it indirectly via Esperanto. The whole ESB and middleware layer could be generated. If this happens, the ESB itself could have a limited life; it could be replaced by a set of utilities that the Brownfield-generated Artifacts could use to route and queue the services as required.

Could the use of Brownfield-generated Artifacts mean the end of middleware? Perhaps. Looking at it in another way, however, the middleware is still there but is provided within Brownfield-generated Artifacts. Middleware in the future could be sold as a set of add-ons for Artifact generation in Brownfield.

Evolving a Deployable Enterprise Architecture

Many large organizations often have sought a complete metadata description of the entire enterprise, yet they have rarely achieved it—and even fewer have managed to maintain such a description. Such initiatives have historically been associated with a Greenfield reboot of core systems. (This technique was particularly popular with data models in the 1990s.)

We come across the remains of such initiatives on a regular basis. Most have failed (often spectacularly) because this involves much work and provides little gain until it is completed. The architects involved have often been accused of sitting in ivory towers (or even, in one case, a gilded ivory tower).

Brownfield reengineering provides a means of producing a formal enterprise architecture in an evolutionary way, producing immediate gains. We believe that VITA—which means "life" in Latin—really does mean the beginning of life for enterprise architectures. The Brownfield development approach and the VITA architecture provide a mechanism for the embodiment of enterprise-level specificity and precision for solution deployment and control—no more ivory towers, high-level building blocks, technology choices, and abstract edicts. Such a view is probably controversial but could well prove justified.

Using Brownfield to build interfaces starts the collection of such data. In fact, by the time Brownfield has been used to generate all the interface configurations on a major project, you will have attained a large part of the goal described earlier: a metadata description of much of the business's important information. However, this will not be achieved by people behind closed doors who work for years to deliver little business benefit. This will emerge as a byproduct of your development process, not some nugatory work carried out by an isolated team. Cherish this data—do not discard it. This is a major asset to your enterprise.

Your business can use this information not just to develop your applications, but to manage and control your enterprise. You can use the information in the Inventory to assess changes to the enterprise. You can use this information to check the ripple effect of changes to your systems, which currently is very difficult to assess. You can also assess new systems or packages in a similar way to see if they are a good fit for the enterprise—not with some high-level study, but with a detailed analysis at the lowest level.

Ultimately, the information in the Inventory and the generation capabilities facilitate not just the initial creation of the deployable Artifacts, but the ongoing maintenance and changes required to those systems to be automatically generated. The enterprise can then truly gain the flexibility that it has always sought. Changes can be accommodated quickly, in a controlled engineered manner, for a known cost.

Your enterprise could change completely—you just have to recognize that it is a Brownfield site and take the first step....

Index

A

Abstract Syntax Trees (ASTs), 171
abstraction, 113, 118, 131
  complexity, 122-124
  complexity example, 121-122
  drawbacks of, 120
  ripple effect, 124-128
  software engineering, 120-121
  systems integration, 113-118
accelerated delivery on Brownfield
  sites, 156-159
Acceptance Phase, Brownfield
  development approach, 163
adding information, 199
agile development methods, 135
agile methods, 144-151
  approach to waterfall problems, 151
  versus waterfall methods, 145
Albrecht, Allan, 16
ambiguity
  Elephant Eaters, consuming the
    environment, 41-43
  Views, 29-30
Anderson, Chris, 102
Architects' Workbench, 187
architecture, 75-76
  abstraction, 118, 122-124
  complexity example, 121-122
  ripple effect, 124-128
  software engineering, 120-121
  Elephant Eaters, 48-49
  Artifacts, 52-55
  Inventory, 50-51
  Transforms, 51-52
  Views, 49-50

precision architectures, merging Views,
  190-194
Artifacts, 198
  Elephant Eater architecture, 52
  consistent configuration artifacts, 53
  documentation, 53
  efficient execution, 53-54
  testing transforms, 54-55
  generating, 198
  paying your own way, 198
  testing, 199-200
assumptions, 124
ASTs (Abstract Syntax Trees), 171

B

Babel Fish, 91-93
Backus, John, 170
Backus-Naur form (BNF), 170
bad news diodes, 8
BAs (business analysts), 140-141
Berners-Lee, Sir Tim, 91, 99, 135
big-mouthed superhero, 40
BNF (Backus-Naur form), 170
Boehm, Barry, 15, 144
Booch, Grady, 90, 104
bottom-up approach to systems
  integration, 113
BPEL (Business Process Execution
  Language), 189
bridging business/IT gap, 79-83
  touring the model, 84-87
  use cases, 79
Brook, Jr., Frederick P., 7, 25
Brooks' Law, 25

Brownfield, 14, 25, 60, 91
CASE, 138-139
death of, 105
deciding to switch from Greenfield,
    xxii-xxiii
evolution, 141-142
legacy code, 170-172
MDA (Model Driven
    Architecture), 139
    business analysts (BAs), 140-141
    evolution, 141-142
moving to, 204
    creating Elephant Eaters, 204-205
    empowering business change, 205-206
    interfaces, 207
site surveys, 20-21
sources of, 134-135, 138
testing, early testing, 156
versus other techniques, 136
VITA, 166
Brownfield Beliefs, 47, 60-61
bridging business/IT gap, 64
embracing complexity, 62
establishing truth, 64
iteratively generating and refining, 63
language, 63
making business and IT indivisible, 61
reuse, 62
Brownfield development
    approach, 158
phases and outputs of, 159-160
subphases and outputs of, 161-162
Brownfield lifecycle, 57-59, 162
Brownfield movement, 168
Brownfield sites, accelerated
    delivery, 156-159
business analysts (BAs),
    140-141, 206
business attractors, 104-105
business change, empowering when
    moving to Brownfield, 205-206

business options, software
    archaeology, 93-96
business process definitions, 67
Business Process Execution
    Language (BPEL), 189
business/IT gap
bridging, 79-81, 83
    touring the model, 84-87
    use cases, 79
Brownfield Beliefs, 64
language speciation, 32-34

C

CAD (Computer Aided
    Design), 75
CAD/CAM (Computer Aided
    Design/Computer Aided
    Manufacturing), 135
CASE (Computer Aided Software
    Engineering), 76, 135, 138
Brownfield, 138-139
change management, risk areas of
    project failure, 9
CHAOS report, xxvi
chaos theory, 105
checkpoints, quality assurance
    checkpoints, 144
choreography, 211
CIM (Computation Independent
    Model), 152
circular references, 178
class diagrams, 169
communication, 25
context, 42-47
formal versus informal, 68
gaps in, 67-72
PowerPoint, 70-72
problems
    language speciation, 31-34
    Views, 26-27
semantics, 42-47
syntax, 42-43

complexity
  abstraction, 121-124
  Brownfield Beliefs, 62
  environmental complexity, 13-16, 18
  effects of, 18-20
  induced complexity, 9-10
Component Model, 68
Computation Independent Model
    (CIM), 152
Computer Aided Design
    (CAD), 75
Computer Aided Design/Computer
    Aided Manufacturing
    (CAD/CAM), 135
Computer Aided Software
    Engineering (CASE), 76,
    135, 138
Configuration Artifacts, 198
considerations for Elephant Eaters
  conflicting goals, 111-112
  interactions, 112
  transparency, 110-111
consistent configuration
    artifacts, 53
constraints, 14-15, 49-50
consuming the environment,
    Elephant Eaters, 41
  overcoming inconsistency and
    ambiguity, 41-47
context, 42
  Elephant Eaters, consuming the
    environment, 43-47
  overcoming inconsistency and
    ambiguity, 43-47
customers, 103-104

D

Data Definition Language
    (DDL), 166
data sources for forming
    Inventories, 168

DDL (Data Definition
    Language), 166
decomposition of complex problem
    space, 118
DeMarco, Tom, 30
developing tools, 207
diagrammatic views, 169
diagrams, 67-68, 71
documentation, 53
Documentation Artifacts, 198
Domain Object Model (DOM), 149
dynamic aspects, considerations for
    Elephant Eaters, 112
dynamic services, 100-103

E

Eclipse, 171
Eclipse Modeling Framework
    (EMF), 187
Elephant Eaters
  in action, 55-57
    generating and refining, 59-60
  architecture, 48-49
    Artifacts, 52-55
    Inventory, 50-51
    Transforms, 51-52
    Views, 49-50
  Brownfield Beliefs, 60-61
    bridging business/IT gap, 64
    embracing complexity, 62
    establishing truth, 64
    iteratively generating and refining, 63
    language, 63
    making business and IT indivisible, 61
    reuse, 62
  considerations for
    conflicting goals, 111-112
    interactions, 112
    transparency, 110-111
  consuming the environment, 41
    *overcoming inconsistency and ambiguity,
      41-47*
  creating, 204-205

environment, 130
portrait of, 200-201
elephant-eating strategies, 39-41
EMF (Eclipse Modeling
  Framework), 187
Engineer Phase, Brownfield
  development approach, 162
enterprise architectures, evolving,
  212-213
Enterprise Service Buses (ESBs),
  209-211
environment, 129
environmental complexity, 13-18
  effects of, 18-19
  ripple effect, 18-20
ESBs (Enterprise Service Buses), 211
  building, 209-211
evolution, Brownfield, 141-142
Executable Artifacts, 198
execution, artifacts, 53-54
exploring Inventory manually,
  73-75
extracting information, merging
  Views, 189-190
extracts, 198

F

function point analysis, 16
functional requirements, 11

G

gaps in communication, 67-72
generating Artifacts, 198
  paying your own way, 199
generation faults, identifying, 200
Gerstner, Lou, 30
globalization, 6
goals, conflicting goals, 111-112
Greenfield, deciding to move to
  Brownfield, xxii-xxiii

H

Haasjes, Geert-Willem, 100
Hilbert space, 72-73
  Inventory, exploring manually, 73-75

I

IBM
  Inventory structures, 179
  patents for implementation of
    Brownfield, 205
  System/360, xxi
IBM islands, 84
IBM Rational Software Architect
  (RSA), 189
identifying
  generation faults, 200
  missing or incorrect information,
    186-187
  patterns, 169-170
IFPUG method, 16
inconsistency
  Elephant Eaters, consuming the
    environment, 41-47
  Views, 27-28
induced complexity, risk areas of
  project failure, 9-10
inference, 190
innovation capacity, IT
  spending, 18
interactions, considerations of
  Elephant Eaters, 112
interfaces
  building, 207-209
  moving to Brownfield, 207
Inventory
  data sources, 168
  Elephant Eater architecture, 50-51
  exploring manually, 73-75
  importers, 57
  OWL, 180, 183

structure of, 173
triples, 173-180
Inventory optimizers, 105
IT, 79
IT spending, 18
iterative development, 93

J-K

JAD (Joint Application
  Design/Development), 135

L

language, Brownfield Beliefs, 63
language speciation, 31-32
  business/IT gap, 32-33
  making business and IT indivisible, 34
languages
  choosing, 205
  ontologies, 98-99
  OWL. *See* OWL
legacy code, 170-172
lifecycles, Brownfield lifecycle,
  57-59
lifetimes, 73
Lister, Timothy, 30
Logical Data Model, 68
Lojek, Bob, 124
long tail, 102

M

mashups, 134
MDA (Model Driven Architecture),
  152-153
  Brownfield, 139
  BAs (business analysts), 140-141
  evolution, 141-142
  Pattern Driven Engineering, 153-154
  reversing, 155-156
MDA/MDD (Model Driven
  Architecture/Model Driven
  Development), 135

MDD (Model Driven
  Development), 64
memory techniques, 67
merging Views, 183, 185
  extracting information, 189-190
  identifying missing or incorrect
    information, 186-187
  precision architectures, 190-194
  time dimensions, 187-189
  transforms, 195-197
metadata, 87
metaphors, 84
Microsoft PowerPoint, 70-72
middleware, 212
Model Driven Architecture (MDA),
  151-153
  Brownfield, 139
  business analysts (BAs), 140-141
  evolution, 141-142
Model Driven Architecture/Model
  Driven Development
  (MDA/MDD), 135
Model Driven Development, 57, 62
models, bridging business/IT gap,
  84-87
mosaic language zones, 32
moving to Brownfield, 204
  creating Elephant Eaters, 204-205
  empowering business change, 205-206
  interfaces, 207
Mythical Man Month, The, 25

N

Naur, Peter, 170
nonfunctional requirements, 11

O

Occam's Razor, 10
OMG (Open Management
  Group), 152
On Demand, 95
ontologies, 98-99

Open Management Group
    (OMG), 152
organization, risk areas of project
    failure, 7
outputs of Brownfield development
    approach, 159-162
OWL (Web Ontology Language),
    138, 180
    Inventory, 180, 183

P

Palmisano, Sam, 95
parable of the blind men and the
    elephant, 24
parochialism, 47
    Views, 30-31
parsing Views, 169-170
Pattern Driven Engineering, MDA
    (Model Driven Architecture),
    153-154
patterns, 125
    identifying, 169-170
Peopleware, 30
phases of Brownfield development
    approach, 159-160
physically separated teams, 30
PIM (Platform Independent
    Model), 152
planning, risk areas of project
    failure, 7
Platform Independent Model
    (PIM), 152
Platform Specific Model (PSM), 152
plumbing, comparison, 121
PowerPoint, 70-72
precision architectures, merging
    views, 190-194
presentations, 71-72
private languages, 32
process flows, 67-68
project reporting, risk areas of
    project failure, 7-8
PSM (Platform Specific Model), 152

Q

quality assurance checkpoints, 144

R

RAD (Rapid Application
    Development), 135
RDF (Resource Description
    Framework), 138, 180
RDF graphs, 183
RDF/XML extract, 180
regulatory compliance, IT
    spending, 18
reporting on projects, risk areas of
    project failure, 7-8
representing triples, 72
requirements
    conflicting requirements, 111
    functional requirements, 11
    nonfunctional requirements, 11
    risk areas of project failure, 11-13
Resource Description Framework
    (RDF), 180
reuse, Brownfield Beliefs, 62
reversing MDA (Model Driven
    Architecture), 155-156
ripple effect, 18, 131
    abstraction, 124-128
    effects of environmental complexity,
        19-20
risk areas of project failure
    change management, 9
    globalization, 7
    induced complexity, 9-10
    organization and planning, 7
    project reporting, 7-8
    requirements, 11-13
RSA (Rational Software
    Architect), 189
rules, 93

S

Sarbanes-Oxley, 18
Second Life, 77
semantic technologies, 90
semantic web, 99-100, 135, 183
semantics, 42
  Elephant Eaters, consuming the
    environment, 43-47
  overcoming inconsistency and
    ambiguity, 43-47
Service Oriented Architecture
  (SOA), 33
services
  customers, 103-104
  dynamic services, 100-103
singing pigs, 70
site surveys, 14, 110, 141, 168
  Brownfield sites, 20-21
skills, developing for Elephant
  Eaters, 204
SOA (Service Oriented
  Architecture), 33
software archaeology, 91-93
  business options, 93-96
  structures, 96-97
software engineering, abstraction,
  120-121
sources of Brownfield, 134-135, 138
splitting, 113
  systems integration, 113-118
Standish Group, xxvi
static testing, 163
steady state, IT spending, 18
Stock, Gregory, 105
stove-pipe systems, 16
strange attractors, 104
strategies for elephant-eating, 39-41
structure of Inventory, 173
structures, software archaeology,
  96-97
subphases of Brownfield
  development approach, 161-162

Survey Phase, Brownfield
  development approach, 162
syntax, 42
  overcoming inconsistency and
    ambiguity, 42-43
System/360 (IBM), xxi, 16
systems integration
  bottom-up approach, 113
  splitting or abstraction, 113-118
  top-down approach, 116

T

TADDM (Tivoli Application
  Dependency Discovery
  Manager), 97, 168
taxonomy, 114
teams, physically separating, 30
Test Artifacts, 198
testing
  Artifacts, 199-200
  Brownfield, early testing, 156
  static testing, 163
  transforms, artifacts, 54-55
text messages, 32
The Open Group Architecture
  Framework (TOGAF), 114-115
three-dimensional displays, 76-78
time dimensions, merging Views,
  187-189
time slices, 73
Tivoli Application Dependency
  Discovery Manager (TADDM),
  97, 168
TOGAF (The Open Group
  Architecture Framework),
  114-115
tool unification, 128-129
tools, developing, 207
top-down approach, systems
  integration, 116
transformations, 195

Transforms
   creating, 197-198
      Artifacts, 198
   Elephant Eater architecture, 51-52
   merging Views, 195-197
   testing, 54-55
transparency, lack of, 110-111
triples, 51
   Inventory, 173-180
   representing, 72
truth, Brownfield Beliefs, 64
Turner, Richard, 144

U

UML (Unified Modeling Language),
   43, 139
UML diagrams, 169
unified tools, 128-129
updating information, 200
use cases, 66, 79

V

Venn diagrams, 99
Views, 26, 166
   communication, 26-27
      ambiguity, 29-30
      inconsistency, 27-28
      parochialism, 30-31
   Elephant Eater architecture, 49-50
   merging, 183, 185
      extracting information, 189-190
      identifying missing or incorrect
         information, 186-187
      precision architectures, 190-194
      time dimensions, 187, 189
      transforms, 195-197
   one-size-fits-all approach, 130
   parsing, 169-170
   software archaeology, 91
   splitting, 114
virtual worlds (v-worlds), 77, 135
   Second Life, 77

visualizations, 87
VITA (Views, Inventory,
   Transforms, and Artifacts), 48,
   166-167

W

W3C (World Wide Web
   Consortium), 179-183
waterfall development, 144
waterfall methods, 146-151
   agile approach to problems, 151
   versus agile methods, 145
Web 2.0, 91
Web Ontology Language. *See* OWL
WebSphere Business Modeler, 187,
   204
World Wide Web Consortium
   (W3C), 180, 183

X-Y

XML, 91

Z

Zachman Framework, 115

BOOKS ONLINE

ENABLED

THIS BOOK IS SAFARI ENABLED

INCLUDES FREE 45-DAY ACCESS TO THE ONLINE EDITION

The Safari® Enabled icon on the cover of your favorite technology book means the book is available through Safari Bookshelf. When you buy this book, you get free access to the online edition for 45 days.

Safari Bookshelf is an electronic reference library that lets you easily search thousands of technical books, find code samples, download chapters, and access technical information whenever and wherever you need it.

TO GAIN 45-DAY SAFARI ENABLED ACCESS TO THIS BOOK:

- Go to **informit.com/safarienabled**
- Complete the brief registration form
- Enter the coupon code found in the front of this book on the "Copyright" page

If you have difficulty registering on Safari Bookshelf or accessing the online edition, please e-mail customer-service@safaribooksonline.com.